SHEM FLEENOR

Ramparts Magazine Muckrakes America

1848 Publishing Company

New York City

ISBN: 9781951231-16-3

TABLE OF CONTENTS

INTRODUCTION

Ramparts Magazine, an American political muckraker that captured the revolutionary zeitgeist of the era, existed from 1962 – 1975. Unlike most of the radical magazines of its day, *Ramparts* was expensively produced and stylistically sophisticated. It was first established in June 1962 by Edward M. Keating in Menlo Park, California. It was originally intended to be a "showcase for the creative writer and as a forum for the mature American Catholic." The magazine declared its intent to publish fiction, poetry, art, criticism and essays of distinction, reflecting those "positive principles of the Hellenic-Christian tradition" that had "shaped and sustained western civilization for the previous two thousand years," and which were, Keating believed, still needed to "guide American Catholics" in an age that had grown increasingly "secular, bewildered and afraid."[1]

---

[1] "Editorial Policy," *Ramparts,* vol. 1, no. 1 (June 1962), p. 3.

But under the editorship of Warren Hinckle, the look and ethos of *Ramparts* evolved, became a monthly news magazine, and moved its base of operation to San Francisco, California, which was an epicenter of the counterculture. Robert Scheer became managing editor and Dugald Stermer was hired as art director.[2] The trio proceeded to turn *Ramparts* into one of the best known and most respected organs of the American New Left.

The New Left can perhaps best be defined as a loosely organized and mostly white student movement that advocated democracy, civil rights and various types of university reforms. The proverbial tie that bound the disparate classes, races, nationalities and ideas associated with the New Left was opposition to the American war in Indochina.

---

[2] Peter Richardson, *A Bomb in Every Issue: How the Short, Unruly Life of Ramparts Magazine Changed America*, (New York, The New Press, 2009).

The term "New Left" was first popularized in the United States in an open letter written in 1960 by sociologist C. Wright Mills. It was titled *Letter to the New Left*. In it Mills argued for a new and improved leftist ideology that he hoped might transcend the traditional and often dogmatic "Old Left" focus on labor issues and subsequent lack of concern for issues such as racism, sexism and the destruction of environment. Mills aimed to encourage a broader focus on issues such as opposing alienation, anomie and authoritarianism. Mills thus argued for a shift from traditional leftism, toward the values of the counterculture and, echoing Karl Marx, emphasized and advocated an international (rather than nationalistic) perspective on the movement. Mills also claimed that the proletariat (collectively the working-class referenced in Marxism) was no longer the revolutionary force in the postwar world; the new agents of revolutionary change in the decades after World War II were, Mills believed, young intellectuals such as college students, scholars and editors of leftist academic books, journals and muckraking publications.

Ramparts, perhaps more than any other American publication of the era, was especially committed to championing the values espoused by Mills. The magazine's editors were acutely attuned to and committed to social movements around the world. Many articles published in *Ramparts* thus either mentioned, explicitly focused on, or published essays contributed to the magazine by several inspirations, influences, key figures and luminaries of the global New Left, including Mills, Albert Camus, Guy Debord, Simone de Beauvoir, Allen Ginsberg, Emma Goldman, Che Guevara, Ho Chi Minh, Vladimir Lenin, Rosa Luxemburg, Herbert Marcuse, Bertrand Russell, Jean-Paul Sartre, Leon Trotsky, Malcolm X, Mao Zedong, Mahatma Gandhi, Stokely Carmichael, Noam Chomsky, Angela Davis, Régis Debray, Tom Hayden, Abbie Hoffman, Huey Newton, Carl Oglesby, Jerry Rubin, Mario Savio, Bobby Seale, Todd Gitlin, Howard Zinn and César Chávez.

The pages of *Ramparts,* in short, read like a who's who of the New Left.

Despite its profound cultural significance, by the time I began research on this project, only one book had been published about *Ramparts* – Peter Richardson's *A Bomb in Every Issue: How the Short, Unruly Life of Ramparts Magazine Changed America* (2009), which was awarded a *Mother Jones* Best Book of 2009 for its outstanding work uncovering the largely untold story of this great American muckraker. Richardson's book delved into the magazine's cultural significance and traced its trajectory from its 1962 birth as a "forum for the mature American Catholic" through its turbulent peak years (1967-1968), to its financially strapped demise in 1975. Richardson also deftly showed how *Ramparts* shaped the counterculture in the Bay Area of Northern California and vice versa. He also juxtaposed *Ramparts* against some of its contemporaries, most notably *Rolling Stone, Esquire* and *Time.* Richardson also drew valuable

connections to the later emergence of
publications such as *Mother Jones.*

As great as *A Bomb in Every Issue* is as an
examination of the external life and times of the
magazine and the middle-class white men at
helm of *Ramparts,* I was, as a historian with a
background in journalism, more interested in the
inner-life of the magazine and the publication's
depiction and coverage of many of the most
seminal events in both American and world
history during the 1960s and early 1970s. In other
words, I was more interested in the magazine as
journalistic history and the magazine's incredible
primary source material.

By the time I began research on this
project *Ramparts* had been fully digitized online.
The digital archive spanned thirteen of the most
turbulent years in world history. It thus provides
an invaluable database of primary source
material with which to get a great sense of how
the American New Left narrated the events that
shaped the Vietnam era in American history,

including the rise and demise of the New Left as a viable political force in the American polity.

The database provides a window into an America in which leftism was actually a viable political alternative and force that seemed to have a profound impact on the nation's culture and political system. By September 11, 2001, there was no viable antiwar movement or rights revolution that was even remotely comparable to the movements unabashedly championed in the pages of *Ramparts*. By the turn of the twenty-first century, both major political parties in the United States were unwavering proponents of American militarism as the cornerstone institution in American life, and neither the Democratic or Republican political parties had programs designed to address the same inveterate racism, sexism, poverty and degradation of the environment that were routinely addressed in the pages of *Ramparts* in the late-1960 and early 1970s. The militarism, corruption, warfare and corporate welfare that *Ramparts* routinely exposed had not, in short, significantly abated in the decades after the end of the Vietnam War; in many cases the economic and political corruption that *Ramparts* sought to expose was far worse at the turn of the twenty-first century than in 1975, when the final issue of *Ramparts* was published.

Ramparts Magazine Muckrakes America examines the muckraking publication's relentless depiction of American society from 1962 – 1975, with chapters focused specifically the rapacious nature of Cold War crony capitalism, the prevalence of poverty, scarcity and want in the midst of what economist Kenneth Galbraith referred to as "The Affluent Society." Other chapters are focused on the publication's depiction of the American Empire's dependence on foreign oil; Law and Order and the weaponization of the American justice system and the rise of the prison industrial complex as a counterrevolutionary force in American society; other chapters chronicle the magazine's muckraking of corporate, political and educational corruption; other chapters focus on the publication's coverage of presidential politics, including the assassinations of John and Robert Kennedy and the Watergate scandal.

CHAPTER ONE

"The Tyranny of Postwar American Capitalism"

Ramparts Magazine published several essays that depicted capitalism as the primary cultural force in Cold War America, which compelled conformity and was the handmaiden of authoritarianism, corruption, inequality and fascism. For instance, in April of 1966, Gene Marine, who had previously written extensively for magazines such as *The Nation,* and was a former news director for *Pacifica Radio,* contributed a story to *Ramparts* titled "Totalitarian Capital with Acanthus." Marine argued that conformity and authoritarianism was part and parcel to American capitalism. To Marine, there was a deep strain in American identity between freedom and authoritarianism. New York City, he argued, was the global capital of capitalism and epicenter of those twin tendencies in Cold War American society and identity. New York City's skyline and the svelte interiors of buildings with their abstract expressionist paintings were, Marine asserted, evidence that capitalism forced conformity without most consumers even realizing it. New York was, according to Marine, a primary source of social discord in Cold War America. "The architecture of New York," Marine wrote, was "crucial to the onset of totalitarianism in America" — not because it reflected it, but because it was among its major causes.[3]

In November of 1970, *Ramparts* published an essay written by Michael Sweeney, who was a member of the Pacific Studies Center. Much of the articled focused on the actions of A.P. Giannini, who crafted Bank of America into what Sweeney described as an empire. From the Wall Street Crash, the Dust Bowl, profiteering during World War II, to driving American involvement in the developing world through the Cold War, Bank of America was, Sweeney elaborated, a protagonist. While praising the glories of free enterprise, Bank of America had, Sweeney asserted, built a monopoly. As the bank went, he

---

[3] Gene Marine, "Totalitarian Capital with Acanthus," *Ramparts Magazine*, April 1966, p. 33.

argued, so went America. Each of Bank of America's successes was built on the misery of what Sweeney referred to as the "little fellows" that the bank erroneously claimed to serve. The bank's profits were, he asserted, taken out of the "hide of the farm worker and distilled from the blood of the Vietnamese." He asserted that no bank was more emblematic of an America that had twisted the "spirit of individualism into the world's greatest nightmare." While enriching the elite of Italian-American immigrants, it impoverished the mass of the Mexican-Americans. While opening up the riches of Asia, it condemned the vast majority of Asians to perpetual poverty. "It was not diabolical scheming that brought these results," Sweeney concluded, "it was success — the kind of success defined by American capitalism."[4] The capitalism fostered by banks too big to fail such as Bank of America, Sweeney concluded,

---

[4] Michael Sweeney, "Bank of America: The "People's Bank" Builds an Empire," *Ramparts Magazine*, November 1970, p. 24.

inevitably bread inequality and sowed the seeds of social despair.

In March 1971, *Ramparts* published an essay titled "Watch Out: Prosperity Is Just Around the Corner (Again)," written by Doug Dowd, who was a Visiting Professor of Economics at the University of California, Berkeley. To Dowd, "prosperity" equated to bankers such as Giannini getting a bit richer to detriment of workers all around the world. He argued that American economists such as Milton Friedman had helped harm the American economy by being beholden to Wall Street rather than workers. After the economy began to move into inflationary trouble in 1967 and into contraction in 1969, each "bad" sign along the way was interpreted by the economists who spoke for the profession and the government as "aberrant," but each "good" sign was seen as significant and profoundly meaningful — exactly, Dowd noted, as had happened with the official reports on the Vietnam War.

In other words, American powerbrokers only recognized good news as actual news. But by 1971, the American economy seemed to be spiraling towards stagflation – persistent high inflation combined with high unemployment and stagnant demand in a country's economy. Dowd realized that stagflation would lead to widespread social suffering and thus recognized it as an opportunity to galvanize the New Left. To become a movement that could substantively change American society in humane directions, Dowd wrote, it was especially imperative that the Movement joined its moral and social concerns to a program that focused on the death-dealing qualities of the American economy — not just for the ghettos and the youth culture, but for all who worked for a living, whether with blue or white collars, and of whatever color or sex or continent. At the very moment when the prospect for such a movement seemed bleakest, it was, for the same reasons, Dowd optimistically asserted, "closer to our reach than ever before." But to fully grasp the opportunity, he concluded, required more work, more seriousness, more humility, more thought and more understanding of American society and its people than either the Old or the New Left had yet put forth.[5]

In May of 1971, *Ramparts* published an essay titled "The Profit Motive and the Public Interest: Wright Patman vs. the Bankers," written by Walter Shapiro, who was a graduate student of history at the University of Michigan and a former political reporter for *The Congressional Quarterly*. Patman was a U.S. Congressman from Texas and a self-styled "populist" who made a name attacking the American banking system and the Federal Reserve system concomitant to advocating decentralized American life (i.e. Main Street values ahead of Wall Street values). To Patman, the greatest enemy of America was the oligarchs "encrusted like barnacles on the hull of the American economic system." But despite Patman's bombast, Shapiro noted, the alternative

---

[5] Doug Dowd, "Watch Out: Prosperity Is Just Around the Corner (Again)," *Ramparts Magazine*, March 1971, p. 44.

to Wall Street was not Sinclair Lewis' *Main Street*, nor was the alternative to Chase Manhattan Norman Rockwell's Americana. And Patman, who had fought the good fight, could not drag the U.S. back to the era of the small and local savings-and-loan personified by George Bailey in *It's a Wonderful Life* (1947) because, Shapiro argued, that version of America no longer existed anywhere in the U.S. The corporations, Shapiro concluded, had a monopoly on America's banking system and thus had a monopoly on all aspects of American life.

In September 1971, *Ramparts* published two essays about Lockheed, the American global aerospace, defense, security and advanced technologies company. The first essay was titled "How the U.S. (and Britain and Germany...) Got Involved in Lockheed," written by Robert Fitch. The second was titled "Lockheed's Life and Hard Times," written by Joel Yudken, who was a former engineer at Lockheed Missiles and Space Company. Fitch, citing a report written by Ralph Nader, the consumer advocate, argued that

Lockheed was the beneficiary of corporate welfare. According to Nader, the loan of First National City Bank, one of the Lockheed consortium, represented either complete oblivion to the economic facts of life or faith in the taxpayers' willingness to bail out the company. It made little economic sense for Lockheed, Fitch asserted, to receive funds from banks to develop a plane that was vastly inferior to those already being developed by Boeing and McDonnell-Douglas. Good sense was, however, Fitch noted, beside the point because much like the American banking industry, Lockheed had grown too big to fail. As such, corporations did not have to make sound business sense because if push came to shove the American taxpayer would ultimately save the corporation from failing.

Yudken argued that financial and investment syndicates began to exert a decisive influence on the growth of the infant industry during World War I. He noted the numerous times Lockheed had faced collapse, only to be saved by bankers before World War II and then again by the federal government during the Cold War. Despite bad management, the increased militarism of American society during the Vietnam War ensured Lockheed's survival. In July 1970, the Senate authorized a $200 million contingency fund as the first installment of government payments to Lockheed in order to keep the company from folding under the weight mismanagement, despite the fact that there was no legal liability for the Pentagon to do so. Both essays about Lockheed published in the September 1971 edition of *Ramparts* underscored the total ownership of the American polity by corporations, especially weapons manufacturers conglomerated with banks.

In April 1972, *Ramparts* published an essay written by Jack Newfield and Jay Greenfield titled "Them That Has, Keep: Taxes." They described a "fair tax system" as one that said to the rich: you will help pay for the schools that will give the children of the un-rich a chance to compete with your children; you will help finance the hospitals to care for the men and women injured in your plants and by your products; you will help pay for the costs of pollution and disease. That was, Newfield and Greenfield explained, what was supposed to happen. But, they lamented, this was not at all how the system worked. The American tax system was, they elaborated, "a fraud" that had been so egregiously and systemically manipulated by the "legal and political hired guns of the rich" that it reinforced, rather than equalized, the power of wealth in America.[6] And, Newfield and Greenfield concluded, the American system had been rigged by the rich for their benefit and to the exploited detriment of everyone else.

Ramparts, also in the April 1972 edition, published an essay titled "Big Sky: Chet Huntley's Home on the Range," written by Frank Browning. Browning focused on the residents of a small town named Ennis Valley in the state of Montana, who were caught in a system of

---

[6] Jack Newfield and Jay Greenfield titled "Them That Has, Keep: Taxes," *Ramparts Magazine*, April 1972, p. 34.

agriculture which enriched big agricultural enterprises to the detriment of the other farmers in the state. "Even if the small farmers being pushed out by agricultural corporations would have tried to expand their farms or ranches," Browning wrote, "they had little chance of success because the recreational speculation fueled by advertisements in national magazines had driven prices up so far that production could not support the higher acreage prices that resulted from large farms and new resorts frequented by wealth Americans such as *CBS's* Chet Huntley, who was also invested in driving real estate speculation in a resort he was invested in named 'Big Sky.'" Small farmers in Montana were thus, Browning asserted, increasingly squeezed out by real estate barons and agricultural corporations. Huntley's endorsement in particular, Browning noted, drew attention to the resort and imbued value in the real estate market, which drove up prices of land. Browning further argued that Montana would become a giant sprawling park, it's "body bared to those affluent enough to escape for a month of leisure each year to their own private hideaways in the most beautiful and rugged corners of the wilderness."[7] Though resorts such as Big Sky fueled development and speculation, Browning concluded, this development was for the benefit of a wealthy few at the expense of the environment and regular Montanans.[8]

In September 1972, *Ramparts* published a review written by Doug Dowd of Andreas G. Papandreou's *Paternalistic Capitalism* (1972). Papandreou wrote from an unusual background; his experience embraced not only the academic world of teaching and research but also the world of political and governmental affairs and his varied career was global in dimension. As a cabinet minister in Greece and a leader of the country's democratic forces, he was imprisoned and then exiled by the military junta which seized power in 1967. He continued the struggle

---

[7] Frank Browning, "Big Sky: Chet Huntley's Home on the Range," *Ramparts Magazine*, April 1972, p. 44.

[8] Ibid, p. 44.

for a democratic Greece as leader of the Panhellenic Liberation Movement. His book provided a critique of American capitalism and its relationship to U.S. foreign policy. Papandreou first examined the orthodox view of the contemporary capitalist economy and what he referred to as the "myth of market capitalism" that it had engendered. He then considered the Neo-Marxist view that the economy could best be understood as monopoly capitalism and the technocratic interpretation of society proposed by J.K. Galbraith. Papandreou accepted and rejected various aspects of these two interpretations and moved to define the salient features of what he referred to as "paternalistic capitalism," wherein privatized decentralized planning was increasingly carried out by the corporate managerial elite, in the interest not of the consumer, but of the "system" writ large.

The paternalism Papandreou described was thus that of an autocratic big brother. He also explored the relationship between the managerial elite and the instrumentalities of the

State and claimed that next to the managerial elite stood the national security managers, which was by no means an accident, for paternalistic capitalism was aggressively expansionist, as was reflected in the foreign policy of the capitalist metropolis, most namely the U.S. The global aspect of paternalistic capitalism was further delineated in Papandreou's discussion of what he described as the "new mercantilism" and of the institutional device of the multinational corporation. Finally, he considered briefly two alternatives — the Soviet experiment, which he rejected as paternalistic socialism, and a vision of a regionally decentralized society, in which humans would control rather than be at the mercy of their social environment. *Paternalistic Capitalism*, Dowd concluded, was an important book that he highly recommended *Ramparts* readers to study and understand.[9]

---

[9] Doug Dowd, "review of *Andreas G. Papandreou's* Paternalistic Capitalism," *Ramparts Magazine*, September 1972, p. 65.

In June 1973, *Ramparts* published an analysis titled "How the U.S. Went Bankrupt," written by Terence McCarthy, who was a consulting economist and Adjunct Professor of Economics at Columbia University. The U.S., he argued, went bankrupt because it borrowed short and invested long, the absolute precursor to bankruptcy, for short-term debts could not be paid out of long-term assets. In 1973 America had $60 billion in net overseas long-term investment, largely financed out of a net-favorable balance of some $90 billion on international trade accounts since World War II. But, McCarthy wrote, the amount of U.S. bankruptcy no longer mattered; whether the foreign official debt was $65 billion or $90+ billion was simply a numbers game because America could not meet its overseas debts — except by new debt and so ad infinitum whatever their real amount.

The reason for American bankruptcy, however, McCarthy noted, mattered very much. Why? Because since the end of World War II the

U.S. had spent $77 billion in direct overseas military expenditures over and above the cost of the wars in Korea and Indochina. Most of this $77 billion—unlike the money spent in actual warfare—had translated into all sorts of short-term debts and obligations upon the U.S., debts which could not be paid out of long-term assets. Moreover, since the end of 1970 and for the first time in the twentieth century, the U.S. had fallen into deficit in her international trade accounts. This was why the U.S., McCarthy explained, went bankrupt. The country simply could not pay her official overseas debts out of her private long-term overseas assets. And it was this bankruptcy which had provoked the inflation that was wracking the country in the early 1970s. In other words, America's Cold War military-industrial-complex economy, which was fostered by the likes of ITT and Bank of America, had sown the seeds for the collapse of the American economy in order to enrich banking corporations and weapons manufacturers at the expense of the average American taxpayer.

In April 1974, *Ramparts* published a sardonic article titled "A Tax Guide for the Rest of Us: If You Can't Give Your Papers to the National Archive...," written by Robert Kaldenbach. His primary advice was to never conceal income, a not-too-concealed jab lobbed at the multinational corporations such as ITT and Lockheed, both corporations of which had made an art of stashing wealth in offshore accounts and thus beyond the grasp of the Internal Revenue Service.

The theme of capitalism being fundamentally flawed and criminally fraudulent appeared again in the July 1974 edition of *Ramparts* in an essay titled "The U.S. Economy: Death of an Illusion," written by Terrence McCarthy. He argued that the nation had committed fundamental errors for which it was time to pay the proverbial piper. The American way by which wealth was measured was deduced, he explained, in the vast deception of the Gross National Product. The greater the waste, he wrote, the greater the wealth. For decades, McCarthy noted, the principal export of the U.S. had been inflation. But this ended in 1973, when foreign central banks declared the American dollar an unwanted asset. McCarthy described the mood in America in 1974 to be one of "general anxiety" derived from "a growing sense that something had gone very wrong with the U.S. and that, whatever it was, lay deep in the foundations of American society and seemed to be worsening.[10]

McCarthy's essay was immediately followed in the July 1974 edition of *Ramparts* by an article titled "The U.S. Economy: The Way Things (Don't) Work," written by Seymour Melman, who was a professor of industrial engineering at Columbia University. His books included *Pentagon Capitalism* (1970) and *Our Depleted Society* (1965). In the article published by *Ramparts*, Melman explained that while Americans landed on the moon in 1969, New York City's infrastructure was breaking down,

---

[10] Terence McCarthy, "The U.S. Economy: Death of an Illusion," *Ramparts Magazine*, July 1974, p. 33.

namely it's power grid, which affected the city's
public services such as the subway system. Many
buildings also lost power for extended periods of
time during a heat wave that summer.
Economists and engineers, he noted, commonly
agreed that competent power supplies,
transportation and communication comprised
the infrastructure of a modern industrial system.
In the absence of such services a country was, he
pointed out, understood to be
"underdeveloped." American industry, its
management, research, production methods and
product design had been held up as a model to
all the world. However, Melman asserted, the
events of 1969 in New York City were but one
fragment of a larger process of deterioration of
American industrial efficiency. Melman seemed
most alarmed by the Department of Defense
vastly expanding the world's supply of
armaments in the early 1970s concomitant to the
seeming collapse of public education in the U.S.
In its quest to declare itself militarily superior to
every other nation, Melman lamented, the U.S.

had seemingly lost its devotion to pursuing idealistic goals. Being superior in both guns and butter, Melman asserted, had been part of the American self-image—guns were even supposed to help make butter… as it has turned out, he concluded, guns had "inevitably taken away from butter."[11] In other words, American warfare had undermined what had previously been positive aspects of American society and character.

In October 1974, *Ramparts* published another essay written by McCarthy titled "Red Ink Capitalism: Banking on Borrowed Time." He asserted that the power of governments to draw savings out of the banking system—to recycle growing public debt as it was due—had suppressed the capitalist ethic of financing industrial growth through personal thrift. But this was, McCarthy argued, "more than an ethic." To capitalism it was a necessity. And the

---

[11] Seymour Melman, The U.S. Economy: *The Way Things (Don't) Work," Ramparts Magazine*, July 1974, p. 39

well had finally run dry. Capitalism, he asserted, could not survive these conditions — and could not change them.[12] By 1974, he noted, a new contradiction had entered the capitalist system. On the one hand, governments outbid private banks on the basis of interest yields. On the other hand, governments rescued big corporations (Such as Edison Consolidated and Lockheed) and commercial banks (such as Chase and Bank of America) if they got into serious trouble. This might, he noted, seem schizophrenic. He, however, demystified this seeming schizophrenia by explaining that capitalism had always presented "two faces." First, as liberator from feudalism and founder of the industrial system, which had immeasurably increased living standards in advanced countries. Second, as ruthless exploiter and despoiler of whoever was too weak to withstand its perpetual attempt to reduce them to bare subsistence and industrial

---

[12] Terence McCarthy, "Red Ink Capitalism: Banking on Borrowed Time," *Ramparts Magazine*, October 1974, p. 29.

servitude. The contradiction of contradictions, in fact, was, McCarthy asserted, that the powers of government, and their means of appreciation created by capitalism to serve the capitalist system, had in fact grown so vast and so oppressive in capability that "capitalism itself had become their subject." The executive committees of the national bourgeoisie had thus become so massive that the bourgeoisie had been subdued by them. Government had thus grown almost all-powerful. The highest probability – if the people permitted it – appeared to be that the government, already a prime borrower and determiner of interest rates, might also become prime lender, making capital advances from the printing press to corporations (directly or indirectly) at its own discretion and in whatever directions the bureaucracies decided. A historically determined process had, he argued, come to an end. Its death throes, he concluded, were not a pleasing spectacle because there was no guarantee that what was to follow what seemed in 1974 to be the final collapse of the capitalist system would be any better than what had preceded it.

Americans tend to think of global politics in terribly provincial terms: one is either a Democrat, a Republic, or at the lunatic fringes of the polity. Americans' political provincialism often prevents them from recognizing that despite how polarized the American polity may seem on the reality television program that is American politics, it is actually quite uniform. The military is such a central part of America's militarized society that American culture dictates that political candidates, regardless of their race or gender, must profess to being God fearing, pro-military, pro-law and order, and dogmatically capitalist in order to stand a chance of being elected. And so, despite the fact that conservative Americans often assail New Deal liberalism to be the spearhead of international socialism, Franklin Roosevelt's New Deal programs actually saved capitalism from collapsing under the weight of its own inherent moral and structural deficiencies. In other words,

New Dealers were not socialists, they were the saviors of American capitalism. In the early 1970s, however, the weight of endless American military campaigns put too much weight on social programs established from the 1930s through Lyndon Johnson's Great Society programs of the 1960s, which was rolled back all through the end of the twentieth century. Robert Moses, whose career was largely shaped by the deficit spending and public works projects associated with New Deal programs, is thus rightly presented in the pages of *Ramparts* to be a metaphor of the state of the corporatist American economy that seemed to be collapsing in 1975.

In March 1975, for example, *Ramparts* published an essay titled "Buildings Are Judgment," written by Marshall Berman, who was an American philosopher and Marxist humanist writer and a Distinguished Professor of Political Science at The City College of New York and at the Graduate Center of the City University of New York, where he taught Political Philosophy and Urbanism. Berman wrote that he was "obsessed" with Robert Moses, who was an American public official who worked mainly in the New York metropolitan area. Known as the "master builder" of mid-20th century New York City, Long Island, Rockland County and Westchester County, he was akin to Baron Haussmann of Second Empire Paris, and was also one of the most polarizing figures in the history of urban development in the U.S. His decisions favoring highways over public transit helped create the modern suburbs of Long Island and influenced a generation of engineers, architects and urban planners who spread his philosophies across the nation. Moses seemed to personify Keynesian economic theory and therefore New Deal capitalism.

The primary questions that puzzled Berman in regard to Moses were: What kind of man was this Moses? What made him tick? Where were the springs of his colossal energy and audacity, his monstrous pride and arrogance, his insatiable will to build up and tear down? Berman compared Moses to other "titanic builders and destroyers" in world history including: Gilgamesh; Louis XIV, the creator of Versailles; Pushkin's Bronze Horseman, the enormous statue of Peter the Great that loomed over the Imperial Capital he had built, and that, generations after his death, menaced Petersburg's citizens and drove them mad; Ibsen's Master Builder; Baron Haussmann, who razed so much of medieval-and revolutionary— Paris, and created what Berman referred to as the "boulevards and vistas of our romantic dreams;" Bugsy Siegel, master builder of the underworld, who created Las Vegas, and was killed for it; "Kingfish" Huey Long; Mr. Kurtz; and Citizen Kane. Bergman also compared Robert Moses to Goethe's *Faust* – an intellectual who sold his soul to the devil in exchange for superhuman powers, but who felt fulfilled only when he gained the power to build, to irrigate and develop an arid and barren coast, to make the wasteland bloom and open it to human life, and to murderously do away with the people in his way. But Berman also mythologized Moses by declaring that his life was a great American epic, of a wealthy German-Jewish immigrant who came to America, and forever changed the nation's nature. In the New York version of this drama, Robert Moses, Berman noted, played a crucial role: he was sitting on top of the world Berman and members of the New Left were trying to topple. Thesis and Antithesis, Moses and the New Left, Berman concluded, needed each other.[13]

In May 1975, *Ramparts* published a series of essays that were counterparts to Berman's titled "Buildings are Judgment II," with essays written by Terence McCarthy, Alan Temko, Percival Goodman, Mary Perot Nichols, John H. Schaar, and a conclusion provided by Berman. In his March 1975 essay, Berman beseeched the New Left to draw out of the Moses experience a new synthesis, a revived sense of the romance of construction that might reconcile the elements of

---

[13] Marshall Berman, "Buildings Are Judgment," *Ramparts Magazine*, March 1975, pp. 33-39

grandeur and humanity of authoritarianism and individual liberty. The question of how this dialectic ought to be defined had emerged by 1975 as the subject of what Berman described as "a provocative and intriguing controversy," from a variety of viewpoints. As such, Part II of "Buildings are Judgment," presented a selection of ideas for transcending the American system Moses had such a heavy hand in building.

The first contribution to the series, published in the May 1975 edition of *Ramparts,* was provided by Percival Goodman, who was a member of the American Institute of Architects, a professor of Architecture at Columbia University, and co-author (with Paul Goodman) of *Communitas: Means of Livelihood and Ways of Life* (1974). Her essay underscored the importance of humanities and liberal arts in an increasingly technocratic and corporatist military industrial complex in which morality took a backseat to economic exigencies. "Who had the moral fiber to look too closely when power, money and concrete achievement were offered?"

she rhetorically asked readers. "Not many," she answered definitively, "and not because these men were lacking in good will. They simply were educated to ask, 'how shall I do it?' but never 'why?'"[14]

The second contribution to the series was written by Mary Perot Nichols, who was a Senior Editor of *The Village Voice* and had written for *Dissent, Cultural Affairs, The New York Times Book Review,* and *Book World.* She noted the creative destruction at the root of Moses central planning. Moses, she asserted, wanted to slum clear places like SoHo, Little Italy and Chinatown, whose cultures were ultimately spared from the wrecking ball and highway. Midtown, which were remade according to Moses' vision, with its high-rises and windswept canyons, had become, Nichols argued, "dehumanized, crime-ridden and dull."[15]

---

[14] Percival Goodman, "Buildings are Judgment---II," *Ramparts Magazine*, May 1975, p. 47.

[15] Mary Perot Nichols, "Buildings are Judgment---II," *Ramparts Magazine*, May 1975, p. 49.

Nichols' article was followed in the series by an essay written by John H. Schaar, who was a political philosophy professor at the University of California, Santa Cruz, and had written for *The New York Review of Books* and *American Review*, and was also the author of *Escape From Authority: The Perspectives of Erich Fromm* (1961). Schaar placed the blame for the fate of American society not at Moses feet. Moses was, Schaar argued, merely "a product of his environment." Moses, Schaar elaborated, "did not create the social forces he served. He did not invent the automobile. At most, Schaar wrote, Moses merely exposed America's "national traits in gigantic characters of stone and steel," thereby revealing Americans to Americans."[16]

Schaar's essay was followed by an article written by Alan Temko, who was the author of *Notre Dame of Paris: The Biography of a Cathedral* (1955), and was an architecture critic for *The San*

---

[16] John H. Schaar, "Buildings are Judgment---II," *Ramparts Magazine*, May 1975, p. 50.

Francisco Chronicle. Temko described Moses as surrounded by men who were by no means titans in the industry and as "jealous" of men whom Temko considered to be true giants of their profession such as Frank Lloyd Wright or Walter Gropius, who Moses considered to be "subversive" and un-American.

The series was concluded by Berman's epilogue. Berman, a neo-Marxist, dedicated his academic career to searching for solutions to the endemic social problems Moses had helped to perpetuate. Berman argued that the New Left owed a debt to Moses for exposing Marxists to fundamental questions that revolutionaries in every industrial society were tasked with confronting, including: What kind of cities do we want to live in? And, what kinds of building really can make our lives better?[17] Though there was remarkable diversity of the interdisciplinary interpretations and opinions regarding Moses'

---

[17] Marshall Berman, "Buildings are Judgment---II," *Ramparts Magazine*, May 1975, p. 53.

life and works presented in the "Buildings are Judgment" series, there was also great continuity. For example, each contributor in the series recognized that Moses was indicative of a crisis embedded in American capitalism and identity that desperately seemed to need addressing, lest humanity would continue down an unsustainable existence that would inevitably lead to social catastrophe.

Oil was even more of a driving force in twentieth century capitalism than Robert Moses or the New Deal. Oil was also the lifeblood of America's increasingly militarized society. *Ramparts* thus depicted oil to be both central to the American Empire and the Cold War. For example, In May 1967, *Ramparts* published an essay written by Adam Hochschild titled "Teapot Dome 1967?" The story noted a recent black-gold rush in western Colorado, Utah and Wyoming. Though the government prohibited corporations from acquiring leases to drill for oil on government land, companies had much greater success acquiring drilling rights for dawsonite on government lands. And, Hochschild explained, if an oil company could get a patented claim which allowed it to mine dawsonite, it almost forced the Department of the Interior to also lease the mining rights for oil. It was thus no surprise to Hochschild that a number of oil companies had some of the largest interests in the new dawsonite claims. Among them were the Ancar Oil Company of Boston, the Liberty Oil Company of Toledo, Ohio, and several oil firms from Texas. The underlying issue at play, Hochschild argued, was the enormous political power of the American oil industry. It was a power that had been matched in American history only by the influence of the great railroads at the end of the nineteenth century. It was a power, Hochschild declared, which manipulated state Houses and Congress with ease. "It must be checked once and for all," he concluded, "before the richest natural resource remaining to the American people passes out of public hands for good."[18]

In November 1969, *Ramparts* published an essay titled "Santa Barbara: Oil in the Velvet Playground," written by Harvey Molotch, who was an assistant professor of sociology specializing in urban ecology at the University of California at Santa Barbara. He wrote about a Union Oil Company's shallow water well that had erupted in the Santa Barbara Channel in January 1968, which caused an ecological disaster, the effects of which were washing up on northern California's beaches a year after the spill. In the ensuing months it became clear to Molotch that even more than petroleum had leaked out from Union Oil's drilling platform. "Some basic truths about power in America had," he wrote, "spilled out along with it."

The oil spill, he further elaborated, provided Santa Barbarans with sharp insights

---

[18] Adam Hochschild, "Teapot Dome 1967?" *Ramparts Magazine*, May 1967, p. 14.

into the ways in which American society was governed and into the power relationships that dictated its functions. He placed most of the blame for the disaster at the feet of Richard Nixon's newly appointed Secretary of the Interior, Walter Hickel, who, Molotch explained, had shady dealings in Alaskan Oil and Union Oil, whose well had ruptured off the coast of Santa Barbara. Hickel had, Molotch explained, initially ordered that drilling be stopped soon after the explosion was first reported. But Union Oil ultimately paid academics to persuade Hickel to announce that the problem had passed and drilling could ensue, which caused even more ecological damage to Santa Barbara's coastline and marine wildlife. As bad as the disaster was, Molotch found in it some cause for optimism because Santa Barbara, a community of mostly devout Reagan Republicans, seemed to be educated as result of the spill that leftist activists were perhaps not as insane as they had previously thought. He was, in short, somewhat glad that liberals and conservatives had suddenly found ground for common cause in Santa Barbara as a result of the catastrophic oil spill and the exposing of Hickel's corruption and cronyism.[19]

In December 1971, *Ramparts* published a tiny blurb of an editorial titled "East Coast Oil" that seemed to predict, if not at least foreshadow, the OPEC Embargo and subsequent economic crisis of 1973 and 1974. Middle Eastern countries were, the editorial noted, increasingly demanding more of a stake in the global oil industry, and the big international companies, which dominated the cartels, were using these demands to pressure the U.S. government. American politicians as such increasingly warned of dangerous dependence on "foreign" oil sources and were clamoring for stepped-up drilling programs on the U.S.'s outer continental shelf to meet the so called "energy crisis."

---

[19] Harvey Molotch, "Santa Barbara: Oil in the Velvet Playground," *Ramparts Magazine*, November 1969, p. 43.

These American politicians, such as Hickel, had particularly wanted to drill in the Atlantic Ocean off the east coast. A consortia of thirty-three companies led by Jersey Standard claimed to have found commercial oil and gas deposits thirty miles off Long Island. North Carolina State waters had by then already been leased, and state geologists reported preliminary drilling in federal waters on the outer continental shelf. The Interior Department, which administered the shelf, planned to lease the Atlantic territories by 1976, and planned to hold preliminary environmental impact hearings in 1972. Drilling off the east coast of the U.S. could, however, *Ramparts* editors explained, produce an international wrangle because choice sites were on the Georgia coast, the center of the international fishing industry, and protests were already being heard about the danger to the fish. Despite the concerns to the ecological that were raised, advocates of offshore drilling gained adherents in the wake of the OPEC embargo in 1973-74 amongst otherwise liberal politicians across the American polity who understood the centrality of oil to American economic and military dominance.

In March 1972, *Ramparts* published an essay written by James Ridgeway titled "Gas Battle of Algiers." In 1969, El Paso reached what it termed a "historic agreement" with Sonatrach, an Algerian national oil and gas company. Under the arrangement, the Algerian company would deliver a billion cubic feet of natural gas in liquid form daily to El Paso Natural Gas. El Paso would then distribute the low-cost gas through its pipeline network. Ridgeway argued that the deal had monumental political consequences for both nations. For Algeria, the deal, which involved more than $1 billion, represented a major step in breaking away the country's developing economy from the oppressive French colonial influence and involving it instead with the U.S., which, at the time, Algeria did not even have diplomatic relations. This step was made possible by the initiatives of the Houston-based gas company, the largest gas utility in the U.S.

and a major international fuels conglomerate. The pact was widely viewed as a forerunner of other deals between developing Third World nations and American-owned international corporations, which underscored the centrality of corporate America to American foreign policy.

In July 1974, *Ramparts* published an essay titled "Everything You Always Wanted to Know About Gasoline (but the oil companies were afraid to tell you)," written by Tom Zeman. Zeman helped to illuminate how deleterious gas was to both nature and humans, which, he noted, the gas companies knew about but these corporations did not care anymore about human life than did tobacco companies. Zeman chronicled the exorbitant profits oil companies made from American consumers per annum. Americans, he explained, wasted $2 billion a year for a higher grade of gasoline than their cars actually needed.[20] Though it only cost oil

---

[20] Tom Zeman, "Everything You Always Wanted to Know About Gasoline (but the oil companies were afraid to tell you)," *Ramparts Magazine*, July 1974, p. 7

companies twelve cents a gallon to get gas from the ground into a driver's tank, they charged more than sixty cents per gallon.[21] Some people, Zeman lamented, living in high auto exhaust areas were also increasingly showing signs of the biochemical abnormalities that preceded lead poisoning.[22] It seemed to Zeman a terrible tragedy that humans had grown so subservient to oil and corrupt corporations who were willing and capable to destroy the planet to serve no real purpose but to make shareholders a bit richer. He, in short, felt that people had a right to know what the gas companies already knew.

As diverse as the articles above are, they each help to illuminate the centrality of Marxist and neo-Marxist proselytizing central to *Ramparts*, which placed a great deal of blame for the pervasive economic and political inequality in Cold War American life at the feet of free market capitalism, which the contributors and

---

[21] Ibid, p. 11.

[22] Ibid, p. 11.

editors of *Ramparts* perceived to be fundamentally rapacious of the poor, of minorities, of women and the environment. And so, as diverse as the New Left was, the glue that tenuously held the movement together into the 1970s was the belief that capitalism was at the root of the exploitation that *Ramparts* was dedicated to exposing, confronting and ultimately destroying.

CHAPTER TWO

"Corporate Corruption in Vietnam Era America"

In addition to depicting capitalism as a fundamentally flawed system that fosters social inequality and injustice, *Ramparts Magazine* published several essays critiquing endemic corruption in the American economic system. American consumerism was fueled by advertising. In April 1967, *Ramparts* published an essay written by Dugald Stermer titled "The Father of Advertising." The story included an image of Nazi swastika above the *CBS* television network logo. Stermer described the advertising industry as falling somewhere between the selling of used cars and child molesting in terms of status and integrity. As account executive, creative director, art director, copy writer and agency president, Stermer wrote, Hitler kept complete control over his agency and client for twelve years, branching out in all directions, until an unfortunate quirk of history felled him. Hitler was, Stermer asserted, virtually, the

"Father of Modern Advertising."[23] In other words, Stermer detects in the American advertising industry the same specter of fascism in postwar American as the same brand of fascism that existed in the Third Reich.

In November 1968, soon after Nixon was elected President of the United States, *Ramparts* published an essay titled "Big Brother as a Holding Company," written by David Horowitz and Reese Erlich. The article depicted the U.S. as a "contract state," which lobbyists crafted to benefit the likes of Litton Industries, which had recently won a huge contract to build ships for the U.S. Navy, which, the authors of the article believed, served as evidence of the commandeering of the American political system by corporations. "The contract state of the postwar world must be viewed as a drastic innovation full of unfamiliar portents," they wrote. Instead of fighting "creeping socialism,"

---

[23] Dugald Stermer, "The Father of Advertising," *Ramparts Magazine*, April 1967, p. 5.

private industry on an enormous scale had, Horowitz and Erlich asserted, become the agent of a fundamentally new economic system which at once resembled "traditional private enterprise and the corporate state of fascism." Litton's modernized shipbuilding enterprise, which had already become the largest producer of automated cargo ships in the world, the authors explained, could still, like the older maritime companies, mark up its price to civilian buyers fifty per cent above the prevailing world market price and have the difference paid by U.S. taxpayers.[24] In short, Litton was evidence of the corporate welfare that became increasingly endemic to the American political and economic system during the Vietnam era in American history.

In December 1968, *Ramparts* published a follow-up article written by Horowitz and Erlich

---

[24] David Horowitz and Reese Erlich, "Big Brother as a Holding Company," *Ramparts Magazine*, November 30, 1968, p. 52.

titled "Litton Industries; Proving Poverty Pays." In it they argued that Litton Industries was a holding company for its decentrally-managed subsidiaries. But Litton was not merely a Beverly Hills address where worldwide profits were mailed to be figured by accountants into grand totals. It was a focal point for an empire's growing economic power which it applied with "consummate skill to the great financial and political levers on Wall Street and Washington." Litton was also at the center of the privatization of the public-school system.

Companies like Litton were, Horowitz and Erlich wrote, planning to subcontract a city's complete school system, claiming to be able to meet whatever contractual standards were set more "efficiently" than local school boards could. This would, the authors noted, be a tempting offer to the often hard-pressed, bewildered city officials whose school systems had been bogged down by almost total impotence. And for the community, dumping the whole complex educational crisis into the lap of Litton's "experts" would seem a blessed relief because like a protection syndicate, business provided security to those who cooperate with it. So as government social agencies struggled for funds, business was increasingly turning into an important force for pushing embattled domestic proposals through Congress, which would ultimately be subsidized by the taxpayer. It was, Horowitz and Erlich concluded, "a rigged win-win scenario for corporations," which were increasingly assuming the role of government by the people for the corporations.

In April 1969, *Ramparts* published an essay written by Horowitz and David Kolodney titled "The Foundations: Charity Begins at Home." The article included a picture of John D. Rockefeller portrayed as a high-priest of a pipeline. For 40 years—from 1872 to 1914—the name of John D. Rockefeller was, the essayists explained, "the most execrated name in American life" and "associated with greed, rapacity, cruelty, hypocrisy and corruption. But by April 1969, Nelson Rockefeller had become a prominent American Politian, narrowly missing out on the Republican Party's nomination to Barry Goldwater in 1964. Nelson Rockefeller later became Vice President to Gerald Ford after Richard Nixon resigned in the wake of the Watergate scandal. Nelson Rockefeller's political ascendance was in part the product of what Horowitz and Kolodney referred to as "the massive beautification program, the political face lifting" of the Rockefeller brand that had taken place in the previous fifty years.[25]

The public image of robber barons like the Rockefellers and of American capitalism itself had, Horowitz and Kolodney explained, been "cleaned up beyond recognition." It had, the essayists asserted, taken a great effort and the subsidized bad memory of history; but the greatest credit was due to the royal families themselves, the Rockefellers and the Fords, who by dint of circumstance and through the devices

---

[25] David Horowitz and David Kolodney, "The Foundations: Charity Begins at Home," *Ramparts Magazine*, April 1969, p. 34.

of their lawyers had turned a new institutional face upon the world, at once benign and inscrutable: the nonprofit and charitable foundation. Horowitz and Kolodney describe these charitable organizations as tax shelters for the new robber barons. They elaborated that the income of the 596 largest tax-exempt foundations was more than twice the net earnings of the nation's 50 largest commercial banks in 1969. The annual income of the Ford Foundation alone exceeded that of the world's biggest bank and totaled almost two billion dollars over the previous 30 years. The Rockefeller Foundation, starting life with $34.4 million in 1913, accumulated over the next half century another $876.2 million — three-fourths of it from stock income and capital gains. These foundations, Horowitz and Kolodney argued, sustained the complex nerve centers and guidance mechanisms for a whole system of institutional power. To a remarkable and not accidental degree, this power had both characterized and defined American society and its relations with the rest of the world in the twentieth century. The Council on Foreign Relations in particular was singled out by Horowitz and Kolodney as an organization which functioned as a crucible of policy formulation on behalf of the corporate ruling class. The CFR, they wrote, set up and directed the Brookings Institution, the National Bureau of Economic Research, the National Planning Association, the Foreign Policy Association, the Twentieth Century Fund, the National Industrial Conference Board and the Committee for Economic Development, as well as a whole bevy of institutions inside the universities, like the Russian Research Centers at Columbia (Rockefeller) and Harvard (Ford and Carnegie) and the Center for International Studies at MIT (CIA, Carnegie and Ford). The foundations had also been primarily responsible for the availability of academic research and scholarship to government (and of course for choosing which representatives of the academy should be granted this access).

In May 1970, *Ramparts* published an article titled "The California Water Plan: The Most Expensive Faucet in the World," contributed by Gene Marine, who had authored *The Rape of America: The Engineering Mentality and the Devastation of a Continent* (1968). The California Water Plan was the state's long-term strategic plan for managing and developing water resources. In California, Marine explained, water was power and wealth. In addition to being an example of taxpayer funded corporate welfare, the California Water Plan was also, Marine wrote, "a carefully drawn blueprint for ecological disaster."[26] He especially lamented what he referred to as the selling off a whole area's precious water supply to satisfy certain high-rollers who were big in the para-politics of state power. The Standard Oil Company, Southern Pacific Railroad, industrial ranching operations, and Bank of America, which was the world's largest commercial bank and also a large

---

[26] Ibid, p. 36.

landowner in California, were, Marine wrote, the primary beneficiaries of the California Water Plan. Bank of America alone, he noted, financed more than half of all California agriculture.[27]

In November 1971, *Ramparts* published an essay titled "H. Ross Perot: America's First Welfare Billionaire," written by Robert Fitch. It featured a cartoon drawing of Perot riding a horse made by IBM. The essay chronicled the endemic corruption in America's medical industry. The liberals, Fitch wrote, knew in 1965 that capitalism in medicine was a "bad mixture." They also knew that the status quo — represented by The Blues and the AMA — was very powerful. It had stopped reform efforts for thirty years. So congressional liberals decided to be practical. Their prescription was: make capitalism in medicine mix better. Give health care away free or nearly free to those who could not afford it — the aged and the indigent. Meanwhile, keep

---

[27] Gene Marine, "The California Water Plan: The Most Expensive Faucet in the World," *Ramparts Magazine*, May 1970, p. 37.

organized medicine happy by letting it administer the new federal programs. It, however, Fitch explained, wasn't long before the health care market broke apart after a storm of profit-taking by organized medicine. So, the next step liberals took was to demand more controls over the program. Computers had to be used to keep doctors and insurance companies from further profiteering.

But liberals still knew that the health care status quo was very powerful, so they let a Blue Cross executive be the chief federal monitor and they let him choose the companies he wanted to have run the computer checks and perform the audits on themselves. In this atmosphere of politically flatulent and unfocused concern with health care costs, Ross Perot rose "like a bag of helium."[28] And just as it took a complete outsider, the former Trotskyist social worker Bernie Cornfield, to exploit the potential of the

---

[28] Robert Fitch, "H. Ross Perot: America's First Welfare Billionaire," *Ramparts Magazine*, November 1971, p. 42.

mutual fund racket to its furthest limits, it took a right-wing anti-communist to exploit the medical welfare program to its furthest limits. H. Ross Perot was, Fitch explained, "a true child of his times and ward of the welfare state." By 1971 Perot, "a hard-core, free-enterprise freak" was the man responsible for administering more of the nation's welfare medical programs than anyone else" and "earned a billion-dollar fortune in the process." Perot was thus, Fitch concluded, at the center of the corruption of American Medicare.

The theme of corporations controlling the American polity persisted in a December 1971 edition of *Ramparts* in an editorial written by James Ridgeway titled "The Anti-Populists." Not since Eisenhower had business enjoyed such freedom of movement, Ridgway explained. At the Federal Power Commission oilmen set gas prices. At the Civil Aeronautics Board airline presidents called secret meetings of the Commission and directed the members how to proceed. Antitrust was virtually extinct,

Ridgeway lamented, and politicians of a populist stripe were "disappearing into the woodwork."[29] Also, devout capitalists such as H. Ross Perot and Ronald Reagan were successfully styling themselves as populists in the television show known as American politics.

The chronicling of the corruption of American higher education continued in *Ramparts* in December 1971, in an editorial titled the "LBJificiation of U.T." written by Frances Lang. Lang provided a short summary of American universities serving as brokerages for industrial and political interests. MIT and Harvard brokered the Route 128 complex, the defense electronics "shuck" of the 1960s. Columbia trustees realty schemes for the upper west side of Manhattan. The University of Chicago was Mayor Richard Daley's political club for the south side. But the University of Texas was, Lang explained, slightly different. It not only was the trough for every enterprising

---

[29] James Ridgeway, "The Anti-Populists," *Ramparts Magazine*, December 1971, p. 6.

Austin businessman, but also more importantly acted as a funnel for the political and business interests of the Texas State Democratic Party, whose personnel floated in and out of the University administration buildings and board rooms.

For many years, Lang wrote, the man who ran the University for the Party was Frank Erwin, who served as Chairman of the Board of Regents. Erwin, who was still a Regent in 1971, was an intimate of Johnson, former Governor John Connally, and the current governor, Preston Smith. Erwin was, Lang explained, Democratic National Committeeman from 1964 through 1968, and when the *Daily Texan*, the student newspaper, accused him of having a conflict of interest, he responded, "the University of Texas is Lyndon Johnson's university." When the newspaper opposed Johnson's decision to bomb North Vietnam, Erwin claimed it had cost the University a million-dollar gift and threatened to abolish its editorial page.[30] Though he was unable to put the student newspaper under regential control, many of his other ventures at U.T. were far more successful. Under his influence, the Regents redefined paid members of the student government as state employees, making it impossible for the student attorney to bring student cases against the University. They also had prohibited University administrators from negotiation with student demonstrators rather than immediately bringing in the police; in 1970 the University passed a ruling that no more than three nonresident members might attend a campus meeting. Erwin was the sole witness to testify before the state legislature against a bill placing three nonvoting students on U.T.'s Board of Regents, and the bill failed.

In the summer of 1970, Erwin summarily fired the Dean of the College of Arts and Sciences, who had occasionally differed from him on campus issues. Several faculty members

---

[30] Frances Lang, "LBJificiation of U.T.," *Ramparts Magazine*, December 1971, p. 8.

resigned in protest over this, but when a state senator demanded an investigation of the affair Governor Preston Smith said he was reluctant to enter into a confrontation with Erwin, a friend of Smith's who contributed to his 1968 campaign. Erwin oversaw the demolishing of homes to make way for new campus buildings, including the LBJ library, and pay-to-park lots. The editorial concluded by elaborating that Frank Ikard, on the Land and Investments Committee of the Board of Regents, and was a U.S. Congressman for years, but by 1971 worked in Washington, D.C. as president of the American Petroleum Institute. He was put in charge of determining how the University endowment was invested and to in charge of directing the spread of the University's financial interests. And the University's most recently appointed Regent was Ladybird Johnson, underscoring the point that U.T. Austin was, as Erwin noted, heavily influenced by the whims of both LBJ and the Democratic Party of Texas.

It took ten years of laborious planning and extensive negotiations to create the mammoth Penn Central Railroad, the largest railroad in U.S. history. When the leviathan was finally born of a merger between the Pennsylvania and New York Central Railroads on February 1, 1968, the event was hailed by some as a great day for railroading. But the baby giant survived only 867 days. The crash of the Penn Central set a new record, this time for the largest bankruptcy the United States had yet seen. In March 1972, *Ramparts* published an article written by Robert Fitch titled "The Love Machine: Sex and Scandal in the Penn Central" that chronicled the intentional Enron-esque collapse of Penn Central. Fitch described a wild scenario of inside self-dealings, corporate pimping of women employees and high-level financial swindling on the part of three principal Penn Central aides. The men were David Bevan, ex-chairman of the railroad's finance committee, General Charles J. Hodge, erstwhile partner in DuPont, and General O. F. "Dick" Lassiter, who used to head up a company known as Executive Jet Aviation, Inc. (EJA), in which the Penn Central held the major interest. But neither the Nixon administration, the Justice Department, the Interstate Commerce Committee and the Security and Exchange Commission moved to prosecute the trio.

Finally, on January 4, 1972, eighteen months after the Penn Central declared bankruptcy, which caused a credit panic that the American taxpayer bailed the banks out of, a Philadelphia district attorney named Arlen Specter handed down indictments against the Penn Central Three. The indictment charged that Hodge, Bevan and Lassiter "conspired in their corporate activities to divert in excess of $21 million from the treasury of the Penn Central for themselves and others." Their activities allegedly "drained the resources of the Penn Central, contributing to its bankruptcy." Nearly all the dealings described were made possible by using other people's money, e.g., money belonging to the Penn Central's depleted pension fund, for which Bevan and Hodge were serving as trustees. Money belonging to the pension fund would be invested in some Penn Central subsidiary, like Executive Jet Aviation, then EJA would begin to deal with companies closely held by Bevan, Hodge or Lassiter. The Penn Central pension fund got pillaged, hurting workers for the Penn Central. Only the Penn Central Three made out well since they held comparatively little stock in the Penn Central itself. Though Hodge, Bevan and Lassiter were blamed for the debacle, Fitch argued that the real responsibility for the Penn Central disaster was at the feet of the board of directors. Few of them, however, Fitch concluded, cared about making the Penn Central into a profitable, efficient rail carrier because they knew the company was too big to fail.

In July 1972, *Ramparts* published an essay titled "This Land is Their Land," written by Larry Cassalino, who worked with the Food, Land and Power Project at the Institute for the Study of Nonviolence in Palo Alto, California.

His essay chronicled corporate welfare in California's agricultural industry. In a recent year, he wrote, five hundred large growers in California's Imperial Valley received $12 million in farm subsidies — or $24,000 each. Meanwhile 10,000 poor, landless residents of the Valley received less than $8 million in welfare payments — or $800 each.[31] Cassalino noted that American taxpayers often paid farmers not to grow things. And the things that were grown were, due to pesticides, often deleterious to soil and living organisms and animals and could potentially increase cancer rates among humans. Cassalino also reminded readers that the notion of agribusiness being more efficient than small farmer operations was often erroneous.

In March 1973, *Ramparts* published a profile of International Telephone and Telegraph's Harold Geneen titled "How To Succeed in Business by Really Trying," written by William Rodgers, the author of *Rockefeller's*

---

[31] Larry Casalino, "This Land is Their Land," *Ramparts Magazine*, July 1972, pp. 31.

Follies: An Unauthorized View of Nelson A. Rockefeller (1966); *Think: A Biography of the Watsons and IBM* (1969); and *Brown-Out: The Power Crisis in America* (1972). Rodgers described Geneen as being driven by "a motivational force that must have been genetic in Alexander the Great, Napoleon, General George Patton, Sammy Glick and not notably absent in Richard Nixon."[32] ITT, Rodgers explained, had many overseas interests while Geneen was at the helm. He was personal friends with then Director of the CIA, John McCone. The CIA not coincidentally helped topple João Goulart in 1964 after he nationalized Brazil's phone lines. McCone went to work for ITT a few years after the CIA-sponsored coup in Brazil. The resultant military dictatorship in Brazil subsequently lasted until 1985. ITT also had some $200 million-worth of investments in Chile. Under Geneen's leadership, ITT funneled $350,000 to Salvador

---

[32] William Rodgers, "ITT's Geneen: How To Succeed in Business by Really Trying," *Ramparts Magazine*, March 1973, p. 33.

Allende's opponent, Jorge Alessandri. When Allende won the presidential election, ITT offered the CIA $1,000,000 to defeat Allende, though the offer was rejected. ITT later financially helped opponents wage the coup that resulted in Allenede's death and Pinochet's dictatorship. On September 28, 1973, an ITT building in New York City was bombed by the Weather Underground for involvement in the September 11, 1973 overthrow of Allende. Geneen, in Rodgers' accounting, seemed to personify the endemic corruption of the American polity and military by multinational corporation such as ITT.

An essay chronicling corruption in big-agriculture was published in the June 1973 edition of *Ramparts* in an article titled "A Vegetarian Manifesto: A Statement," written by Frances Moore Lappé, who was the author of *Diet for a Small Planet* (1971). She rejected the oft proffered notion by meat industry executives that there was a "protein shortage" in the U.S. She explained that America was in 1974 a nation consuming well beyond its protein needs with a diet geared to a protein source that was the most protein-costly of all to produce—namely beef. Most Americans in 1974 ate two times their recommended daily protein allowance. She noted the environmental impact of meat production was wasteful and a contributor to global food scarcity. She further argued for environmental vegetarianism — practicing a vegetarian lifestyle out of concerns over animal-based industries and the production of animal-based products. If the meat industry was, she wrote, the prime beneficiary America's obsession with eating meat, then the people of the poorest nations on the planet were the biggest losers. The nutrients were, she concluded, available to provide an adequate food supply for all mankind, but the realities of the world economic system insured that the fat would get fatter and the undernourished would go hungry. It was this system which, she argued, "must be changed" if the world's food problems were to be solved, and with it must change the "American fixation on meat."[33]

Lappé's article was immediately followed in the June 1973 edition of the magazine by an essay titled "Beefed Up: Drugs in the Meat Industry" contributed by Daniel Zwerdling, who was a Washington-based journalist whose articles had appeared in various publications, including *Saturday Review* and *The New Republic*. "If you think there's a drug problem on the city streets," he wrote, "visit your local chicken house or cattle feedlot."[34] He described 2700 various drug compounds euphemized as food additives pumped into Americans' beef and poultry. We can expect more drugs in the future, he concluded, perhaps from the other 60 animal drug producers, which will automatically tenderize the meat while the animal was still alive; regulate estrus so every animal comes into heat at exactly the same time; and perhaps most

[33] Frances Moore Lappé, "A Vegetarian Manifesto: A Statement," *Ramparts Magazine*, June 1973, p. 36.

[34] Daniel Zwerdling, "Beefed Up: Drugs in the Meat Industry," *Ramparts Magazine*, June 1973, p. 37.

spectacular, a new drug which would grow chicken-sized turkeys. It was, he wrote, "all part of a headlong technological rush which, unchecked, could revamp the old maxim: one man's meat is the same man's poison."[35]

Ramparts continued the theme of widespread corporate corruption in the February 1974 edition of the magazine in an essay titled "Payola – As American as Apple Pie," written by Andrew Kopkind. Writing soon after Columbia Records fired Clive Davis for rumors that he had engaged in systemic payola schemes, Kopkind noted the hypocrisy of Davis' firing, citing numerous other recent and more egregious scandals in which executives, such as the Board of Trustees at Penn Central, had gone unpunished. Kopkind's contention was that artsy and liberal executives like Clive Davis were railroaded when corporatists such as Geneen at ITT could quite literally get away with murder due to their CIA connections.

---

[35] Ibid, p. 41.

Ralph Nader was arguably the greatest opponent of the endemic corporate corruption that existed in the U.S. during the 1960s – 1970s. In March 1974, *Ramparts* published an article titled "Ralph Nader: How Far Can a Lone Ranger Ride?" written by William Greider, a reporter on the national staff of *The Washington Post*. Greider's profile of Nader was very positive, depicting him as an idealistic crusader defending American consumers from the corporations who cared only of profits and thought little of public safety. Greider, however, noted that Nader's main tactics were fast becoming antiquated and did not faze corporate lobbyists and litigators who seemed to be rolling back many of the principled victories Nader had won against the likes of General Motors in 1960s. Nader, Greider lamented, had far less success trying to break up the energy monopolies in the 1970s.

In June 1974, *Ramparts* published an essay titled "Lockheed: The High Cost of Dying" which continued the theme of corporate welfare commonly broached in the pages of the magazine. The article was contributed by A. Ernest Fitzgerald, a weapons-cost analyst from Alabama who had blown the whistle on Lockheed, whose executives had intentionally misled the government in cost estimates for C5A transport plane in order to line the pockets of shareholders to the tune of $2 billion at the expense of the American taxpayer. Fitzgerald seemed genuinely concerned about a pattern of corporate corruption that seemed to increasingly be endemic in the American polity.

In October 1974, *Ramparts* published an essay titled "Buying Power: Towards a Public Utility Network," written by Thomas Brom, who was a consultant for the Community Ownership Organizing Project in Oakland, California, and Edward Kirshner, who was an urban and economic planner who was also associated with the Project. They hailed the more than thirty public power systems that had been formed in the U.S. since 1960. They, like Nader, advocated a new public power movement "in the spirit of the radical populists who began municipal systems in the 1880s."[36] Public power would, they explained, costs less and municipal power systems proved that public enterprises could be efficient and profitable for the public. Plus, public systems established during the "mood of disgust" with energy monopolies prominent in the mid-1970s would, the essayists believed, be expressions of community power and proof of the vulnerability of the corporate giants. By itself, Brom and Kirshner conceded, pubic power was not likely to transform the nature of American society overnight. But the thirty publicly owned power systems already working were, they believed, great examples of community control that might be an important adjunct to wider political programs. It was, they concluded, "a beginning step toward revitalizing public energy as an alternative to continued corporate abuse."[37]

---

[36] Thomas Brom and Edward Kirshner, "Buying Power: Towards a Public Utility Network," *Ramparts Magazine*, October 1974, p. 38.

[37] Ibid, p. 30.

Brom and Kirshner's essay was followed in the October 1974 edition of *Ramparts* by an essay written by Peter Collier, who criticized *CBS* anchors Dan Rather, Eric Sevareid, and Walter Kronkite for failing to be objective in their coverage of the new American President, Gerald Ford, who had taken the reins after Nixon's resignation. Collier noted the eagerness of *CBS* to put the Vietnam era and Watergate constitutional crisis behind the country in the interest of restoring some order to the political and economic status quo. Ford, or course, especially irked both liberals and many conservative by later offering a full pardon to Nixon, who had drastically expanded America's war in Vietnam and created the constitutional crisis associated with Watergate, underscoring the point that the American polity had been rigged to serve the interests of political and economic elites.

In December 1974, *Ramparts* published an essay titled "The Advertising Council: Selling Lies..." written by Bruce Howard, who was a reporter for *The Washington Star-News* and had been published in *New York Magazine, the New York Daily News,* and *Change Magazine.* Howard wrote of the Advertising Council, a non-profit corporation funded and directed by America's "bonafide Captains of Industry" who had access to a half-billion dollars of free advertising per year. The council produced campaigns on behalf of American industry and the executive branch of the federal government. Campaigns such as those about the dangers of smoking marijuana and being more productive for employers were depicted as being "in the public interest." The Ad Council was by far the largest advertiser in the world. Since its formation in 1941, the council had used more than $7 billion worth of free "public service" advertising donated by television, radio, newspapers and magazines.[38] Organizationally speaking, Howard explained, the Ad Council had a "Freudian triumvirate — a superego-public conscience, a single-minded id

---

[38] Bruce Howard, "The Advertising Council: Selling Lies..." *Ramparts Magazine,* December 1974, p. 25.

(the Industries Advisory Committee), and an ego (the decision-making board of directors) that, in this case, curiously resembled the id." The fourth, and not so silent partner of the Ad Council's board was, Howard elaborated, the federal government, which often used the council as a champion for its various projects. Of the council's twenty-five major campaigns each year, more than a third were associated with boosting and popularizing government projects. The campaigns ranged from peddling low-interest U.S. Government Savings Bonds, to pushing recruitment for the National Guard and the Armed Forces Reserve, to promoting the Justice Department's anti-crime campaigns in 1971-72. Howard took issue with the power of the Ad Council and the business interests it propagated to shape public opinion. In the last two hundred years, he wrote, "power in the United States had shifted slowly but inexorably to big business and big government."[39]

---

[39] Ibid, p. 32.

Howard's article was followed immediately in the December 1974 edition of *Ramparts* by an essay titled "...And Selling Truth," written by Henry Weinstein, who was a member of the California Bar and whom also wrote for *The New York Times*. The tenor of the essay was similar to Brom and Kirshner's call for public ownership of power. Weinstein, however, advocated public control of entities such as the Ad Council, which could be used for the public good, rather than the promotion of government funded programs that benefited the interests of economic elites such as H. Ross Perot and multinational corporations such as IBM and ITT. Weinstein noted the establishment of Public Interest Communications, which was created to make content that opposed the Vietnam War. Weinstein's article seemed to encourage readers to explore their own options for turning the tide of endemic corporate corruption that existed at all levels of American society, most especially the polity, which had been overrun by corporate lobbyists and litigators.

Ramparts Magazine, as the previous chapters have illuminated, was a muckraking monthly headed by an editorial staff dedicated to exposing the endemic corporate corruption part and parcel of American capitalism. Capitalism had, the magazine proffered time and time again, undermined American democracy. The endemic corporate and political corruption part and parcel of American capitalism was also, as the next chapter helps to elaborate, not just at the root of undermining American democracy, but also central to keeping America's poor mired in poverty.

CHAPTER THREE

"Organized Labor's Corruption"

Ramparts Magazine published several stories championing the American labor movement. Several stories, however, also depicted endemic corruption amongst labor leaders who were, some essayists found, had been bought off by corporations. Other essays describe organized labor unraveling along racial lines. In March 1966, for instance, *Ramparts* published an essay titled "The Strike that Nobody Understood," contributed by Gene Marine, who was a New York City labor writer, whose articles had also been featured in *The Nation*. "The Strike that Nobody Understood" chronicled the 1966 New York City Transit Worker Union strike, which led to the passage of the Taylor Law, which redefined the rights and limitations of unions for public employees in New York.

The TWU's leader, Mike Quill, who had been the Union's president since the organization was founded in 1934, initially led the striking workers. The strike effectively ended all service on the subway and buses in the city, affecting millions of commuters. The strike was also, Marine believed, an "ominous" beginning for the mayoralty of John Lindsay, but was perhaps most remembered for the jailing of Quill and for his death by heart attack only weeks afterwards. Part of the reason nobody, as Marine put it, understood the strike was because of the one-sided and negative coverage that denigrated the strikers. Marine lamented that both *The New York Times* and Mayor Lindsay undermined the workers' actions and, Marine insinuated, killed Quill.

In April 1967, *Ramparts* published an editorial titled "How the CIA Makes Liars Out of Union Leaders." The Central Intelligence Agency, the editors argued, "saw the American unions as a perfect group to manipulate." The editors noted that the union leaders who allowed their organizations to be used as fronts for the CIA were people who were once among the very best of American liberals, including Arnold

Zander of the American Federation of State, County and Municipal Workers. Zander's role vis-à-vis the CIA, the editors lamented, "explained more about the failure of American liberalism than it did about the CIA."[40] The acceptance by American trade union leaders of an anti-communism which the editors of *Ramparts* asserted no longer had "any relevance to the realities of world politics and national life" was, to them, glaring evidence that the internal life of American unions was in dire need of revitalization, and that union leaders needed to stop treating their members "as if they could not be told about the real world." Union members were, the editors asserted, often actively duped into supporting policies propagated by union leaders in league with the CIA, which often actively undermined the interests of the global, including American, working class. This was, the editors concluded, the "corrupting effect of the CIA in American life." The CIA, in short, made

---

[40] Ibid, p. 28.

union leaders into "liars," which made union members mistrust their elected officials and thus had done a more effective job of destroying the belief of American workers that their unions existed to defend their interests and not the interests of other parties."[41]

In November 1968, just days after the general election, *Ramparts* published an essay titled "'Scab' Teachers," written by Sol Stern. In he, Stern chronicled The New York City teachers' strike of 1968, which was a months-long confrontation between the new community-controlled school board in the largely black Ocean Hill–Brownsville neighborhoods of Brooklyn and New York City's United Federation of Teachers. The strike dragged on from May 1968 to November 1968, shutting down the public schools for a total of thirty-six days, which, Stern explained, increased racial

---

[41] Ibid, p. 28.

tensions between Black and Jewish New Yorkers in Brooklyn.

The UFT was 55,000 strong in 1968 and probably the most powerful white-collar union in the country. The ethnic makeup of the teachers union, Stern explained, which was two-thirds Jewish, had led to an exaggerated perception in the black community of the UFT being simply a "Jewish union." And cooperating with the union during the strike was the Council of Supervisory Associations, which represented all principals and assistant principals. It was also predominantly Jewish.

In a school system where more fifty-five percent of the children in 1968 were non-white, it was, Stern wrote, "little wonder that there was a sense of inequity, and that black and Puerto Rican parents and activists were trying to get a little more say about their kids' educations, in the same way that the Jews of thirty years earlier also felt compelled to confront the resistance of the Irish who then dominated the school system." By 1968, the high proportion of Jewish names among the organizations in direct conflict with the black community had enflamed what was, Stern asserted, basically a "black-white dispute into even uglier racial overtones." And to its discredit, Stern added, the teachers union, particularly its president, Albert Shanker, fanned the flames by sensationalizing the issue of anti-Semitism in order to solidify and rally support from the powerful New York Jewish community.[42] In truth, Stern lamented, most of the replacement teachers hired were also white and Jewish, which discounted notions that black parents were against the union because they were supposedly anti-Semitic.

Stern's also underscored the increased political rift between African Americans and Jews and a gradual but growing conservatism of Jewish Americans in New York City at a moment

---

[42] Sol Stern, "Scab" Teachers," *Ramparts Magazine*, November 17, 1968, p. 17.

when education was increasingly privatized, which was a reaction to the passage of *Brown v. Board of Education of Topeka, Kansas*. Stern's essay is also instructive in the sense that he, who was a Jewish advocate of organized labor, keenly understood that the actions of self-interested UFT members were actually quite deleterious to the American labor movement as a whole because it alienated and disenchanted black and white middle- and working-class folks along racial lines. "Obviously," Stern admitted, there was anti-Semitism in the ghetto and some of it was directed at teachers. He, however, warned readers that a community could not be made sensitive to those concerns by "fiat or by police power." He concluded by explaining that if the union had fought for strong decentralization with adequate legal safeguards for the rights of teachers, and had they cooperated with the local governing board at Ocean Hill-Brownsville in making decentralization work, they would have been better positioned to "protect their members in the ghetto." As it was, Stern concluded, the union's behavior had "undoubtedly increased anti-Semitism in the ghetto and increased the black community's contempt for the average union teacher."[43]

Later in November 1968, *Ramparts* published an editorial titled "The Dodge Rebellion." In it the editors hailed the popularity of Black Power concomitant to criticizing entrenched racism in Detroit's auto industry. The editorial introduced readers to The Dodge Revolutionary Union Movement (DRUM), whose organizers had been inspired by Malcolm X and Frantz Fanon. DRUM was formed in the spring of 1967 at the Hamtramck Assembly Plant, also known as Dodge Main. The plant was located in the midst of a predominantly Polish community; and while 10,000-member Local 3 was more than sixty-percent black, the local had been run primarily in the interests of the remaining Poles and the community of Hamtramck.

---

[43] Ibid, p. 24.

All-black DRUM was, however, attempting to show black workers how union contracts, grievance procedures, meetings and the whole organizational structure could, the editors wrote, "be rigged to sell them out." The local leadership played on the initial reactions of white workers who called DRUM a group of "reverse racists."[44] That was, the editors believed, ironic considering that after a wildcat strike in the summer of 1967, the Polish management fired seven black workers for their actions in the strike; the United Auto Workers won reestablishment for five of the fired, but refused to fight for the other two, who were DRUM leaders.

DRUM then attempted to elect a trustee to Local 3. They backed the candidacy of Ron March, who advocated black unity, black awareness and black identity. The Hamtramck Police Department, which was, in the editors'

---

[44] *Ramparts* editorial staff, "The Dodge Rebellion," *Ramparts Magazine*, November 30, 1968, p. 12/

estimates, not too terribly dissimilar to the infamous Pinkertons, in league with United Auto Worker leadership, colluded to suppress DRUM and derail March's candidacy. March, however, led the balloting with 563 votes, sixty more than the candidate who came in second. When the polls had closed, the editors explained, about fifty DRUM supporters gathered, first in a parking lot and later at the local, to await the returns; police swarmed the union hall, beat and sprayed several DRUM members with mace and arrested others. A week later, March faced a runoff election. Police, however, arrested DRUM members and closed off parking lots of precincts to suppress DRUM, and March ultimately lost the election.

Also in November 1968 – eleven months after Woody Guthrie's death – *Ramparts* published a profile of the famed folk singer written by Pete Seeger and Jo Schwartz. Guthrie was a longtime and especially articulate champion of labor unions such as the AFL-CIO. He was both a leftist and an all-American singer-songwriter, and arguably one of the most significant figures in American folk music. Guthrie also inspired a generation of songwriters that helped provide the soundtrack to the 1960s, including Bob Dylan, Phil Ochs, Johnny Cash, Pete Seeger, Jerry Garcia and Bob Weir; all of whom acknowledged Guthrie as a major influence. Guthrie frequently performed with the slogan "This Machine Kills Fascists" displayed on his guitar. One of his more famous songs of the World War II era included the chorus "All You Fascists Are Bound to Lose."

In October 1969, *Ramparts* published an essay titled "The ILGWU: Fighting for Lower Wages," written by Michael Myerson. His essay chronicled the 450,000-member International Ladies' Garment Workers' Union. The ILGWU's submissiveness on wages and the Vietnam war, Myerson explained, sprang both from the same ideological root: the idea of labor's common interest with business, not only, he wrote, as management, but also in the "global role of imperial agent and anti-communist crusader."

He argued that David Dubinsky of the ILGWU and Matthew Woll of the American Federation of Labor often "undermined" the power and potential of the American labor movement via their conservatism and belief in capitalism as a salutary alternative to communism. "Trade unionism," Dubinsky once sneered, needed "capitalism" like a fish needed "water." Dubinsky and Woll, Myerson explained, also formed a core of anti-communist militancy in the AFL (and later the AFL-CIO). Both men, Myerson believed, carried out a tradition popular during World War II, "labor peace," during the Cold War while business looked toward further imperialist adventures abroad.[45]

The theme of the American labor movement being undermined by devout capitalists in positions of power continued in the January 1970 edition of *Ramparts*, which published an essay titled "Crisis in

---

[45] Michael Myerson, "The ILGWU: *Fighting for Lower Wages" Ramparts Magazine*, October 1969, p. 55

Construction," contributed by The Pacific Studies Center, which was a non-profit research cooperative. The essay included an image of tuxedoed barons (fat cats) pulling the strings of workers as if giant puppet masters.

The article began by describing "Black Monday" demonstrators, including "non-violent civil rights traditionalists, ghetto militants, black craftsmen and contractors, NAACPers, white clergymen, suburban housewives, students and even a few businessmen," all of whom were depicted as marching and singing through the late-summer streets of Seattle, Chicago and Pittsburgh. The marches did not, the essayist found regrettable, inspire racial solidarity amongst many white workers, many of whom asserted that they would stage a "White Friday" counter-demonstration. In the 1960s, the American economy boomed but inflation was also on the rise. So the "average" American worker was by 1971 taking home about a dollar less an hour in real purchasing power than in 1961. Rather than blaming a complex economic system, many white workers, such as those portrayed by The Pacific Studies Center, had a penchant for blaming minority workers, or new hiring quotas, rather than directing their ire at the industrialists or the astronomical costs of funding the Vietnam War.

In September 1970, *Ramparts* continued the theme of America's imperial wars systemically undermining organized labor in an essay titled "Workers Against the War," contributed by Al Richmond, who was a former editor of *The People's World*. The confluence of jingoism towards the Vietnamese and racism towards black civil rights activists was, Richmond explained, especially conspicuous in the building crafts, but not confined to them. Racism and jingoism was, he argued, the "major ideological obstacle to a viable rank-and-file movement" and ultimately made workers closer allies of their employers than other working class Americans. The American Labor Movement was thus, Richmond explained, egregiously undermined by scores of its own rank-and-file members.

This nationalistic and racist idiocy, Richmond asserted, underscored the need for an effective challenge to racism and imperialism in the American Labor Movement. But such a challenge was, he warned, unthinkable without the reemergence of a cohesive left or radical wing in the movement. A potential base for it existed, he explained, in the proliferation of rank-and-file caucuses throughout the country, black caucuses of varying degrees of militancy, and others of even more variegated character, shaped by local needs and circumstances. He concluded by hoping, perhaps naively, "that Nixon's Cambodian incursion may have hastened such a development."[46]

In June 1972, *Ramparts* published an essay titled "The Great American Pension Machine," contributed by Charles Leinenweber, the author of *Power Without Politics: Class Rule in America*

---

[46] Al Richmond, "Workers Against the War," *Ramparts Magazine*, September 1970, p. 32.

(1967). Leinenweber found that Chase Manhattan, which was headed by David Rockefeller and was the nation's third largest pension manager, with more than $7 billion worth of the funds, had "played fast and loose" with workers' pension funds in order to do business with Resorts International, which was run by retired-gangsters.

General Motors' white-collar workers, he explained, put up fifty-thousand Pan Am shares to trade with Resorts — without even knowing it. The company's production workers put up seventy-five thousand shares, also with no knowledge of the transaction. Ford workers contributed one-hundred and thirty shares, a sum matched by Western Electric and Standard Oil of New Jersey. Top honors, however, Leinenweber rued, went to Westinghouse workers, who offered one-hundred and ninety shares. "The workers of Ford and Westinghouse, and all the thirty-two million would-be pensioners covered so "hazardously by the American pension system," Leinenweber wrote, "represented a new breed of philanthropists." Their contributions were, he lamented, directed not toward the poor, but toward the rich. Without remorse, he explained, they gave over their collective life savings to the wealthy, to the Mellons, the Rockefellers, the du Ponts, to the nation's most powerful banks. Theirs was, Leinenweber added, a generosity so vital, that empires could be built on it. It was a generosity unmatched in history. Never had so many given so much to so few.[47] In other words, the American pension system had been rigged by America's most wealthy to ensure that they got even more wealthy than they already were from the labor of American workers, and without those workers even being aware of the risk involved to their retirement funds.

In September 1972, *Ramparts* published an essay written by Staughton Lynd titled "Unions Give Peace a Chance." In it Lynd chronicled a

---

[47] Charles Leinenweber, "The Great American Pension Machine," *Ramparts Magazine*, June 1972, p. 36.

recent United Auto Workers meeting held soon after David Livingston (the Secretary-Treasurer of the Distributive Workers of America), Harold Gibbons (the Midwest Vice-President of the International Brotherhood of Teamsters), and Clifton Caldwell (the Vice-President of the Amalgamated Meat Cutters and Butcher Workmen) had returned from Vietnam. The conference may well have marked a step forward, Lynd explained, but it remained to be seen whether or not the step was really a significant one. The future of Labor for Peace was, he concluded, problematic because its survival and effectiveness would ultimately depend on its ability to devise a concrete program of action and to affect a real democratization of its structure. If not, he warned, it would remain "little more than a coalition of union leaders," which, was ultimately what happened.

In November 1972, *Ramparts* published an essay titled "Japanese Colonialism in Appalachia," written by James Ridgeway, who was working on a book about the energy industry. Appalachia, as Ridgeway rightly noted, had a long history of grinding poverty and capitalist exploitation of the region's workers and mineral resources. Ridgeway's essay seemed to add a new and previously ignored chapter to the history of Appalachian exploitation. He noted the irony of an Asian power, Japan, exploiting what he referred to as "the American heartland" a mere generation after the conclusion of World War II.

He then explained that The Marshall Plan was not just an aid package that salvaged the economies of Japan, Germany, and other places ravaged by World War II; it also put American corporations in business with capitalists (many of which were unabashedly fascist before and during World War II) from the defeated nations. This, he added, created new avenues of exploitation for multi-national conglomerates to explore in places such as Appalachia.

The joint U.S.-Japanese venture in Coal Country U.S.A. in the early 1970s was, Ridgeway explained, only feasible because it was so profitable. Those profits depended on the "skein of existing colonial policies," which, throughout Appalachia, ensured that property taxes remained low, safety and health laws remained lax, and labor remained relatively cheap and exploitable. Those policies, the historic cause of poverty in Appalachia, made U.S. coal competitive with the coal mined in South Africa.

There was also, Ridgeway pointed out, deeper irony to the situation. U.S. workers in the coalfields were exploited to produce coal that was shipped to Japan, used to make steel and other products, and then re-imported into the U.S. to undercut more expensive products (such as cars) made by other U.S. workers in places such as Detroit. In a very real sense, Ridgeway explained, by tolerating the conditions in Appalachia, the U.S. labor movement was, he lamented, "cutting its own throat." In a narrower context, the same companies which had promoted the energy crisis (i.e. Continental Oil, Occidental Petroleum, etc.) in the early 1970s, were themselves contributing to that crisis through direct export of fossil fuels, and by directing production away from U.S. markets, where the prices were not judged to be sufficiently high, to more lucrative foreign markets.[48]

In December 1972, *Ramparts* published another essay contributed by Lynd titled "Conversations with Steelmill Rebels." Racism was again a prominent theme in Ohio, which undermined organized labor's collective bargaining power. A worker named John Barbero, for example, underscored a conservative backlash palpable on the shop floor in the early 1970s. He explained to Lynd that racism seemed worse than ever, which had the effect of dividing the local, thereby diminishing worker solidarity and power.

---

[48] James Ridgeway, "Japanese Colonialism in Appalachia," *Ramparts Magazine*, November 1972, p. 19.

In June 1974, *Ramparts* published an essay
titled "Trying to Stay Alive: Collective
Bargaining in Brooklyn," written by Jonathan
Maslow, who was a freelance writer based in
New York City. Maslow chronicled the bitter
contest between a small Army Supply company
named Do-All with their union (Local 107). He
noted that Big Labor was not the largest part of
the American Labor Union and pointed out that
it was in fact comprised mostly of small unions
and companies, rather than the AFL-CIO and
UAW, which had tens of thousands of members.
If these small unions were more activist and
revolutionary, Maslow asserted, they could
"overpower the larger unions," which, he
regretted, increasingly seemed to be selling out
the labor movement.[49]

Also in June 1974, *Ramparts* published an
essay titled "Miners for Democracy: Year One at
the UMW," written by Ward Sinclair, who was

---

[49] Jonathan Maslow, "Trying to Stay Alive:
Collective Bargaining in Brooklyn," *Ramparts
Magazine*, June 1974, p. 20.

chief of the Washington Bureau for *The Louisville Courier-Journal* and *The Louisville Times*. Sinclair had covered the coal industry and the United Mine Workers for several years. In "Miners for Democracy: Year One at the UMW," he described the UMW of Appalachia as outraged that one-hundred thousand of their brothers had been killed in the mines in the twentieth century, outraged over black lung and more than 1.5 million disabling accidents since 1930, and outraged about the union-financed murder of Jock Yablonski. The UMW was also outraged at callous government and wanton corporations ignoring them and worse, outraged over their own leaders pillaging the union treasury, "whoring with company sweethearts and managing their affairs with dictatorial style."[50]

But there was more to it than that, Sinclair explained, and when these rank-and-file Miners

---

[50] Joseph Albert "Jock" Yablonski was an American labor leader in the United Mine Workers in the 1950s and 1960s. He was murdered in 1969 by killers hired by a union political opponent, Mine Workers president Tony Boyle. His death led to significant reforms in the union.

for Democracy, as they called themselves, swept Tony Boyle from the union presidency in December 1972, underdog unionists everywhere took heart. For here, Sinclair elaborated, were "genuine blue-collar men, guided by no other cause than justice, sweeping away the yoke and crying 'Enough.'"[51]

Sinclair profiled the Miners for Democracy (MFD), a cadre of reformers headed by Arnold Miller, a West Virginian who suffered from black-lung disease. But the organization's power was, to Sinclair's dismay, diminished significantly by mine companies closing shops and heading west to open new operations in states more hostile to unionization, such as Montana and the Dakotas. Instead of "dancing to the corporate tune," Sinclair rued, the UMW had missed an opportunity to exert influence on Congress to restrict the westward tide by writing a strip-mine law that would have forced the industry to more thoroughly internalize its costs

---

[51] Ward Sinclair, "Miners for Democracy: Year One at the UMW," *Ramparts Magazine*, June 1974, p. 37.

and equalize the economic imbalance with deep mining.

The result could have been, Sinclair believed, a "new impulse" for underground mining. But when Congress took up the strip-mine issue in 1973, the reformed UMW had less and less to say about it. "Sadly," Sinclair conceded in spite of high-minded efforts by MFD, reform was ultimately undermined by UMW's conservative leadership, and thus what had seemed to be the dawn of a new era with the workers taking control of the means of production was ultimately throttled by union leadership who seemed to increasingly share a greater affinity for the capitalists who exploited workers than the workers they supposedly represented.[52]

In September 1974, *Ramparts* published an essay titled "Workfare: How Rhetoric Met Reality and Lost," contributed by Tom Zeman. In it Zeman wrote about the Community Work Experience Program, which Ronald Reagan had

---

[52] Ibid, p. 57.

referred to as the "cornerstone" of his welfare program, and which the presidential candidate hoped to make a steppingstone to the White House. Zeman described it as a work-for-a-welfare-check program, which normally recruited people for work assignments such as filing or stuffing envelopes, by threatening to cut off their welfare payments if they refused. Zeman explained that destroying welfare was central to Reagan's rise from a two-bit actor to political cult figure.

Reagan had, Zeman explained, successfully seized upon a rhetoric of "welfare chiselers," which was as effective an epithet as "campus rioters" and "crime in the streets" for getting out the vote from Eureka to Orange County, California. In 1971, after a meeting at San Clemente with Richard Nixon, the latter offered Reagan the services of the Department of Health Education and Welfare in the interest of implementing a large-scale demonstration of Governor Reagan's plan to derail welfare.

Reagan's people, Zeman lamented, soon took over HEW in 1973 and began to "ram his CWEP program down the throat of California's welfare recipients in the hopes of selling it as a model of national reform as a presidential candidate in the 1976 primary." Reagan, in short, envisioned the transformation of the welfare system into an employment preparation system. Reagan's plan was, however, Zeman noted, more expensive than welfare because the successful cases of welfare-to-work programs had traditionally been on-the-job training projects such as those associated with programs, which provided able-bodied welfare recipients with real jobs; provided the medical care, daycare and whatever else was needed to allow them to work; and then provide training on the job.

Such programs were, Zeman explained, very expensive because they not only committed a government to creating new jobs, but also would eventually force the government to provide daycare and medical facilities for others besides former welfare recipients. That would mean a commitment to a full employment economy, which in turn would require radical changes in the structure of the economy itself. The solution for Reagan was to set up such a system that did not actually train people for jobs, did as little as possible in support services such as childcare, transportation, and medical and rehabilitative services, and did not create any new jobs – only more poverty and dependency.

Though *Ramparts* was a mouthpiece of the New Left and thus fully committed to championing the rights of workers, the essays chronicled in this chapter illuminate that organized labor was under a severe but often overlooked assault all through the 1960s and especially during the 1970s. What is perhaps most illuminating about many of these essays is the effect class and race had in undermining organized labor. The racism of workers undermined solidarity and collective bargaining power, and individualistic union leaders often considered themselves to be a higher social class than the workers they supposedly represented, which further undermined organized labor's ability to be a viable political force in a militarized society and empire in which poverty was increasingly depicted by cult figures such as Reagan to be the fault of the exploited rather than part and parcel of American capitalism.

CHAPTER FOUR

"Poverty in The Affluent Society"

Ramparts Magazine published several stories about the rapacious nature of capitalism and the endemic corruption in American corporations and political system. *Ramparts* also published several stores about America's poverty-stricken victims of the inherent inequality endemic to American capitalism during the 1960s and early 1970s. In December 1965, for example, *Ramparts* published an essay titled "Death In Kentucky," written by David Welsh. He chronicled the dire indigence in Appalachia and explained The Appalachian Regional Development Act of 1965, which was meant to be a pillar of President Lyndon's Johnson's War on Poverty. In the 1960s, one in three Appalachians lived in poverty. Per capita income in the region was twenty-three percent lower than the U.S. average, and high unemployment forced millions to seek work outside Appalachia. In 1965, Senator Jennings Randolph (D-WV) introduced a Johnson-backed

Appalachian aid bill calling for more than $1 billion in federal assistance to the region. The Public Works Committee reported the bill to the Senate on January 27, 1965, and the Senate passed the bill on February 1, 1965, with a vote of 62-22. The Act established the Appalachian Regional Commission, which was tasked with overseeing economic development programs in the Appalachia region, as well as the construction of the Appalachian Highway Development System.

The specter of inveterate American poverty and inequality was featured in the May 1965 edition of *Ramparts* in a special report written by John Beecher titled "The Shame of the Cities: McComb, Mississippi," which included photos contributed by Michael Alexander. Like Lincoln Steffens sixty years prior, Beecher engaged in muckraking with a moral indignation aroused by economic inequality in order to rouse Americans to the unwelcome duties of citizenship rather than remain indifferent to a level of corruption that ran so deep that nobody, even the victims of it, seemed to notice. Beecher presented McComb, Mississippi – the town where Students For Nonviolent Coordinating Committee voter registration work had started four years earlier – as a microcosm of the strains of hate, prejudice and ignorance that, Beecher believed, corrupted virtually every segment of American society. Life for the poorest in McComb was, Beecher explained, marred by privation, starvation, uninvestigated murders, and a general cheapness of existence comparable to the Third World. What was, however, in Beecher's assessment, most shocking was not that these things were so common in McComb and many other quarters of the richest nation in the history of the world, but that the people, the citizens of the cities where such things were most common, knew it, but accepted it as simply the way things were rather than revolting against such systemic oppression. Poverty had, in other words, stripped many folks in McComb, Appalachia, and numerous other unmentioned places throughout the United States of their humanity and any semblance of revolutionary potential. Beecher, however, concluded his essay somewhat optimistically by declaring that in July 1965 SNCC was to send out a call for draft resistance to young black people in McComb in an effort to instill a sense of revolutionary agency.

In February 1966, *Ramparts* published an editorial titled "The Poor Get Poorer," which included illustrations provided by Benedict Kocian. The editors asserted that in some parts of the country, high unemployment and low income for both whites and non-whites remained unchanged in any significant way either by the real war in Vietnam or the "not-so-real" war against poverty. Very little, if any, the editors lamented, improvement had been made in the bad housing which was such an affliction of the poor, nor had the much-vaunted Operation Headstart of the previous summer been continued at a significant rate. It was clear, the editors wrote, that the basic problems of poverty for the present generation of the poor and the next few generations to follow would not be solved in traditional ways. "We are facing a grave internal crisis," they declared, "which must not be obscured either by the minimal War on Poverty being conducted nor by the gains to the economy" that had come through the war in Vietnam. In America, they explained, the really poor were only getting poorer while the rest of the population improved its lot. And the solutions for this problem was, the editors asserted, the creation of socially useful public works programs; the relaxation of the rigid standards which controlled hiring; the realization that ordinary fiscal methods could not be applied overnight; and, finally, the understanding that political turmoil was worthwhile if it energized the poor into trying to change their own conditions — these solutions demanded, the editors declared, as much or more effort than was being expended in winning the war in Vietnam. It was, the editors asserted, a tragic flaw in American national character structure that the majority of American citizens viewed a

$50 billion defense budget as a necessary expenditure, but resisted spending an equal amount of money on a program of socially useful public works and activities. Yet nothing less than such a program, they concluded, in which the poor would have an opportunity to make significant decisions about their own future, would have any effect upon those people who continued to live in poverty even though the war in Vietnam escalated.[53]

As flawed and fraught with difficulties as President Lyndon Johnson's War on Poverty was, Richard Nixon's administration significantly rolled back Johnson's initiatives and social programs, which were designed to lift Americans out of indigence. In December 1969, *Ramparts* published an essay titled "Nixon's Guaranteed Annual Poverty," which was contributed by Linda Hunt, Gary Hunt, and Nancy Scheper with research provided by the Southern Rural Research Project, which was a

---

[53] *Ramparts* editorial staff, "The Poor Get Poorer," *Ramparts Magazine*, February 1966, p. 3.

civil rights legal organization the authors had worked extensively with in the black belt of Alabama. On August 8, 1969, in response to the growing volume of criticism of the country's welfare and food programs, President Nixon announced his proposals for reform. His new plan aimed to do away with the main category of welfare, "Aid to Dependent Children," and replace it with a "National Family Assistance Plan" that would retain the food stamp program but would exclude from it those eligible for aid under the new program. The benefits of family assistance would go to the working poor as well as to the unemployed; to families with dependent children headed by a father, as well as to those headed by a mother. A basic federal minimum would be provided, which was to be the same in every state: a family of four with no outside income would be given $1600 a year, an amount which could be supplemented by the state if it chose to do so.

In Nixon's view, this new program might have encouraged welfare recipients to find work by allowing them to keep the first $60 they earned each month without reducing their benefits; beyond that, the benefits would be reduced by fifty cents for each dollar earned. The plan also included a work requirement: those who accepted benefits, for instance, would have to accept job training or work. The only exceptions would be those unable to work and mothers of pre-school children. The proposal even provided an incentive to these mothers in the form of a major expansion of day-care centers. Manpower services would also be state and locally controlled. Nixon had termed this decentralization the "new federalism." Mayors and politicians from large urban centers were, however, quick to complain that the new family assistance program was designed to alleviate the problems of rural America, while doing nothing significant to salvage America's sinking cities, whose tax bases had been systemically wracked by white flight suburbanization in the decades after the conclusion of World War II.

Governor Nelson Rockefeller of the state of New York, allying himself with Mayor John Lindsay of New York City, complained that the states which had done the most to help those in need would receive the least benefits under Nixon's new federalism, which was, Senator Abraham Ribicoff of Connecticut declared, great for places such as Alabama and Mississippi, but it did nothing to help his state alleviate the inveterate poverty that existed in cities such as Hartford. And Senator Jacob Javits of New York stated that while the Nixon proposal would make a major difference in many poor states, especially in the South, it would have little effect in New York. Despite its inadequacy for the northern and urban sector of the nation, the consensus seemed to be that rural America — particularly the former Confederacy — which the Republican Party was actively wooing via the Southern Strategy, had everything to gain from the new program.

The authors of the essay thus focused mostly on the entrenched rural poverty in the

South, which seemed to be an entirely different nation from the urban ghettos of the North, where the poor, the authors of the essay noted, stood a far better chance of enjoying public services (such as public transport) and stood far better chances of finding gainful employment than did poor southerners. The authors ostensibly argued that the inveterate poverty in places such as Appalachia, Mississippi, and Alabama could never be significantly addressed unless there was a significant redistribution of wealth rooted in a fair, just, and peaceful transfer of land ownership away from the white absentee landowners and into the hands of those who had actually toiled on the land for generations, namely the black tenant farmers whose ancestors had been promised forty acres and a mule at the conclusion of the American Civil War. "The black American wants nothing less than his birthright," the essayists argued, "a meaningful place within a viable economic system that allows him control over his own destiny."[54] Welfare did not, unfortunately, permit poor people control over their destinies in either the rural south or urban north. Only careers and land ownership would, the essayists concluded, provide a far better opportunity for poor Americans to significantly improve their lots in life.

In April of 1971, *Ramparts* published an editorial in its "Hard Times Section" about the Nixon administration's proposal to replace welfare with cash payments of $2000 annually, less than half of what it cost to eat at bare existence. This was, the editors explained, a vicious and crippling Catch-22 for America's poor. Nixon wanted a revenue-sharing system as a means of reforming welfare. For a Federal program, the idea of revenue-sharing was simple: the Government collected taxes, at which it was very astute, and shared a small part of these taxes with state and local governments,

---

[54] Linda Hunt, Gary Hunt, and Nancy Scheper, "Nixon's Guaranteed Annual Poverty," p. 69.

which were, the federal government argued, more effective at identifying day-to-day needs of its citizens. The corollary to the revenue-sharing proposal was that elected officials, not appointed bureaucrats, would be tasked with deciding where tax money ought to be spent.

It was Nelson A. Rockefeller who first championed the idea for revenue-sharing moving, which was, he argued, a move inspired by necessity. On the morning of his fourth and last election as Governor in 1970, he met with his top staff members and learned that New York State faced in its next fiscal year with $1 billion deficit. But he did not want to cut services or raise taxes again. It dawned on him that the only solution was the Feds' revenue-sharing program. Rockefeller thus agreed and embarked on a campaign to convince President Nixon to make revenue-sharing a major presidential goal. First, Rockefeller flew to Sun Valley, Idaho, the resort where the thirty-two Republican governors had gathered for a meeting and retreat, and persuaded even a skeptical Ronald Reagan to endorse a proposal for a $10 billion-a-year program. Rockefeller personally delivered the resolution to Nixon on January 15, 1971.

It was, however, too costly, the President replied, but he agreed to consider an experimental program that Rockefeller could ultimately support. Dejected, Rockefeller then talked to Vice President Spiro T. Agnew, who went back that afternoon and sold Nixon on a $5 billion-a-year program. To make the commitment stick, Rockefeller sent word to the White House that without revenue-sharing the President could not count on New York's 41 electoral votes in the 1972 election cycle. In his State of the Union Message a fortnight later, Nixon made revenue-sharing "the major thrust" of his domestic program. The idea provoked stiff and bitter opposition from a formidable but disorganized coalition of House liberals who wanted to spend Federal money their way and conservatives who wanted to spend no money at all. The House Minority leader Gerald R. Ford promised 120 Republican votes and, at the right time, delivered them. It took sixteen months for revenue-sharing to make it through the House. In the Senate, it breezed through in weeks. Nixon signed it in high campaign style at Philadelphia's Independence Hall, two weeks before Election Day. Revenue-sharing was, the editors wrote, a success from the beginning because big cities in the north got a boost and small-town America could for the first time count on direct aid from Washington.

There were also no strings on how the money could be used, and the oversight requirements were simple. Every community had to hold public hearings on how the money would be spent; there could be no discrimination in its use; public audits would show how it had been spent. It was, the editors hailed, government at its finest: elected officials were given resources and authority and held accountable at the next election for what they had done. Revenue-sharing's overhead was also low: a phenomenal one-tenth of one percent, on average, for administration, as against eighteen percent for food stamps. Revenue-sharing, however, died in 1986, a victim of the mounting Federal debt and a Washington tradition of preaching intergovernmental cooperation while practicing every-government-for-itself. After October 1986, eighty percent of America's small towns, which were too small to mount expensive lobbying campaigns for grants from the huge Federal bureaucracies, would be disfranchised in terms of direct financial aid from the Government.

In May 1972, *Ramparts* published an essay titled "Eating It! From Here to 2001," contributed by Judith Van Allen, who was the co-author, with Gene Marine, of *Food Pollution, The Violation of Our Inner Ecology* (1972). She argued that the pollution crisis was both an internal and external matter and inevitably pervasive in a capitalist society. In January 1970, the Institute of Food Technologists announced "SOS/70" — an effort to get food scientists and food technologists to focus their skills on making famine extinct. That same organization presented its annual food technology industrial achievement award to General Foods' Cool Whip — a non-dairy whipped topping. Cool Whip, Van Allen explained, was mostly water, sugar and vegetable oil, with gums and emulsifiers to make it stick together, and artificial color and flavor to make it taste "even better" than whipped cream. It also had almost no nutritional value. And of course, Van Allen noted, it was packaged in white molded plastic containers. "So much for the starving millions," she sardonically quipped.[55]

The futuristic food about which the food technologists dreamt, she explained, was not the inexpensive, protein-, vitamin- and mineral-rich food needed by the poor. Food technologists, she lamented, much preferred technological "miracles" such as Cool Whip as opposed to healthy nutrition. She described these food "miracles" as "fabulous something's made out of

---

[55] Judith Van Allen, "Eating It! From Here to 2001," *Ramparts Magazine*, May 1972, p. 26.

nothing with a good profit margin," designed for purchase by the overfed affluent – and by anyone else who could "be conned into buying them."[56] She included the ingredients to consumer products such as Sweetarts Candy, Chee-tos, and Dream Whip to underscore the chemical compounds that comprised these so called "miracles" that set the stage for the catastrophic rise in rates of obesity amongst the American poor in the waning decades of the twentieth century.

In May 1972, *Ramparts* published two more essays that chronicled American poverty. The first was titled "Seattle: The New Poor Face the New Depression;" the second was titled "The New Poor: A Case Study." Jon Stewart, a free-lance journalist who decades later became host of Comedy Central's *The Daily Show*, wrote both essays. He depicted Seattle as having a long history of boom and bust cycles stretching back to the 1890s, the time when the railroad first arrived. By 1972, the timber industry had,

---

[56] Ibid, p. 26.

Stewart explained, all but collapsed due to over-exploitation of the resource, which left large swaths of poverty-stricken and broken families in its wake. Boeing had also recently laid off 67,000 workers in the region in the previous three years, which created a Great Depression-like scenario for the Pacific Northwest. The net result, Stewart wrote, was that thousands of families, which only two or three years prior were living comfortably and securely, in $30-50,000 homes, and driving two late-model cars, and buying $15,000 pleasure boats and vacation homes in the country, were by May of 1972, living off food stamps or free food provided by a non-profit organization called Neighbors in Need, and gradually selling off their prize possessions to meet mortgage payments (except, of course, for the 4033 families whose homes had already been reclaimed by the Federal Housing Administration).

It was, Stewart explained, a whole class of poor people, designated by the Senate Select Committee on Nutrition and Human Need as the

"New Poor." To a considerable degree, Stewart wrote, their problems were different from those of the "old poor." Their assets, those they had managed to hold on to, disqualified them from any of the Public Assistance programs the government provided the "old poor." What little income these newly christened members of the "new poor" managed to scrape together, after their savings were gone, came mostly from unemployment benefits, and those were fast running out. Many of them were still trying to maintain mortgage payments on their homes and keep up monthly payments on automobiles. But far too often, Stewart lamented, there was not even money left after the monthly payments to meet the price of food stamps.[57] The American Dream had thus, Stewart concluded, come and gone for the "new poor" in Nixon's America.

The theme of the "new poor" was likewise prominent in the December of 1972

---

[57] Jon Stewart, "The New Poor: A Case Study," *Ramparts Magazine*, May 1972, p. 52.

edition of *Ramparts* in an essay titled "Who Goes Begging in America?" written by Richard Parker, who had served as a Junior Fellow at the Center for the Study of Democratic Institutions and as an intern economist at the United Nations and also as an editor of the *Santa Barbara (Calif.) News and Review.* 1972, Parker noted, was a time when the American Middle Class seemed to be disintegrating and the Affluent Society of the 1950s when the nation had the world's largest Gross National Product and the world's highest per capita income than the rest of the world combined, and when Americans ate better, dressed better, received better educations and better medical care than any other people in the world, and lived in better homes in nicer communities, enjoyed more leisure, and traveled more widely than anyone else seemed a distant memory. By the close of 1972, it was, Parker lamented, hard to find anyone who held such a completely sanguine vision of American prosperity. The Sixties, he explained, had reintroduced conflict on a massive scale: war, assassination, riot, and rebellion filled the pages of newspapers. The deaths of a president, a presidential candidate, and a major civil rights leader, plus the deaths of nearly 50,000 Americans in battle were, he lamented, landmarks of the previous decade. Widespread poverty and even malnutrition had likewise been rediscovered in American society, dealing a heavy blow to the image of homogeneous affluence.

To be sure, he wrote, there was affluence in America, but it was "sharply limited for the vast majority."[58] Since America, in fact, was not an Affluent Society, let alone an opulent one, since malnutrition and poverty coexisted with enormous wealth, and since the middle class was a term which increasingly described a family that was only one step ahead of poverty or a family one step short of riches, the question of economic equality remained as crucial in 1972 as it was to

---

[58] Richard Parker, "Who Goes Begging in America?" *Ramparts Magazine*, December 1972, pp. 29.

Thomas Jefferson and Thomas Paine in the early years of the Republic. Exposing the myth of the middle class did not, Parker argued, show how Americans might achieve that equality, but it did support what stood in its way. A solution was, he noted, lacking because it required not new ideas, but new will and that will, Parker argued, needed to come from the majority itself. Returning equality to the vocabulary of Americans was, he concluded, only the first step; whatever further steps were taken, only the American people would decide.[59]

In April 1973, *Ramparts* published an essay titled "Confessions of a Single Mother: A Personal Protest," written by Susan Griffin, who lived in the San Francisco Bay Area, and was a writer, poet and teacher. Griffin penned her article to give voice to women who were raising children on their own. The illusion, she wrote, persisted in 1973 that the nuclear family was "normal" even though only thirty-five percent of

---

[59] Ibid, p. 29.

the nation's population lived in nuclear families. In fact, the number of families headed by women was, she noted, rising more rapidly than the number of all families. "But," she lamented, single mothers were "still pariahs" and their economics were "marginal. The needs of single mothers were, she explained, not met nor even acknowledged.[60] The fact that there was no subsidized childcare made matters even more difficult for single mothers and underscored the inveterate gender inequality rooted in American society that second-wave feminists such as Griffin critiqued in her article. In the final analysis, she wrote, "any society must be judged in terms of the way it treats its weakest, its most vulnerable members." The U.S. was," she reminded readers, a world power, "run by and for the benefit of a minority — grown-up white men who complain louder than all the children in the world about a meager welfare program while they themselves steadily waste the world's

---

[60] Susan Griffen, "Confessions of a Single Mother: A Personal Protest," *Ramparts Magazine*, April 1973, p. 41.

resources in pollution and warfare. We can," she concluded, "only judge such a society as a failure."[61]

In May 1973, *Ramparts* published a report written by James Ridgeway titled "The War on Poverty, Nixon Pulls Out." Ridgeway chronicled Howard Phillips' dismantling of the Office of Economic Opportunity, an outfit he had previously described as "Marxist." Ridgeway seemed to revel in reports that OEO workers openly ignored his orders and routinely leaked any and every memo to the press in attempts to undermine Phillips' systemic dismantling of the OEO. The OEO locals, as Ridgeway called them, had also taken strong stands against America's war in Vietnam, sought to oust various Nixon poverty officials, and tried to build a union among beneficiaries of the poverty programs. They were, Ridgeway argued, "the closest thing

---

[61] Ibid, p. 44.

in the federal government to a radical union of public workers."[62]

In August of 1974, *Ramparts* published an essay titled "Purgatory on Wheels," written by Eugene Meyer, who was a *Washington Post* reporter who covered urban affairs. Meyer's articled starkly contrasted the utopian propaganda and advertisements that prominently hailed mobile home parks as the cornerstone of American life. Gerald Ford, for example, before a mobile home manufacturers' meeting in Washington in 1974, said that the trailer park industry epitomized "the free enterprise system."[63] Meyer agreed. But he, unlike Ford, did not see this a positive thing. Meyer found the gaunt and pale face of American poverty at mobile home parks, what he referred to as the "tin-Can Suburbia" scattered at the periphery of American cities such as the

---

[62] James Ridgeway, "The War on Poverty, Nixon Pulls Out," *Ramparts Magazine*, May 1973, p. 18.

[63] Eugene L. Meyer, "Purgatory on Wheels," *Ramparts Magazine*, August 1974, p. 34.

nation's capital. The U.S. had an enormous
housing problem, Meyer explained, that
extended far beyond the American poor. Interest
rates and construction costs were, he noted,
pricing what little new housing was being built
beyond the reach of even middle-income
Americans. As such, the recent upsurge in 1974
in mobile home construction was, he wrote,
almost certain to continue. And as it did, he
hoped, the growing constituency of mobile-home
owners was very likely to become a force that
legislators could not afford to ignore.[64]

In September 1974, *Ramparts* published an
article that first appeared in *Civil Liberties Review*.
The essay was titled "The Rise and Fall of
Welfare Rights," which was contributed by
Richard A. Cloward and Frances Fox Piven.
Cloward was a sociologist, social worker, and
professor at Columbia University. Piven, was a
political scientist at Boston University. A
collection of their essays, *The Politics of Turmoil:*

---

[64] Ibid, p. 38.

Poverty, Race and the Urban Crisis (1974) had also recently been published. They argued that the liberalization of welfare in the 1960s was a fast fading political phenomenon. Stimulated by the activism of the civil rights movement, the black poor began to question who really was to blame for their plight. The sheer numbers of people enduring the same misery, the essayists argued, made traditional American explanations of poverty more unconvincing than ever. African Americans thus by 1974 increasing began to blame the American system itself, which was rooted in white masculine supremacy of the American economy and political system. The masses who had remained quiescent, despite their travails in the 1950s, increasingly rose up in protest in the Sixties, which was, the essayists noted, a time of marches and demonstrations, of sit-ins and riots. "This explosion," the authors wrote, "and the conciliatory responses by government to it, resulted in a transformation of the patterns that had made possible the wholesale denial of public benefits and of elementary civil liberties in the 1950s and decades prior."[65] But by 1970, the essayists lamented, the political forces that had led to the liberalization of welfare practices began to run their course, and a reaction began to build significantly. Ghetto protests subsided, partly because many people had at least gotten the concession of a relief check, and partly because the most active elements in the ghetto population – the leaders and agitators and organizers – had been quieted by another concession; namely, the availability of jobs in government, in business, and the universities.

Most important, to Coward and Piven, national political opinion was shifting to the right.[66] The essayists then provided readers with the following rhetorical questions: What prospects were there then for more long-lasting reform? And, can the legal basis of the welfare

---

[65] Richard A. Cloward and Frances Fox Piven, "The Rise and Fall of Welfare Rights," *Ramparts Magazine*, September 1974, p. 22.

[66] Ibid, p. 24.

system be reconstructed so as to ensure that the constitutional rights of the poor were to be observed, even at times when the poor remained acquiescent and therefore powerless? Coward and Piven then suggested that guaranteed income schemes such as the negative income tax might be the best method of reform. And that by establishing uniform national grant levels and uniform criteria of eligibility to be administered by a national agency, these proposals could ensure the poor a minimal right to income and limit state and local discretion. Thee essayists, however, lamented that the political climate of mid-1970s U.S. seemed to be bending in the opposite direction, towards "reform by abolishment" of the system entirely. It was, therefore, they concluded, doubtful that any force short of mass unemployment, and then only if it was accompanied by unrest among the unemployed, could fully turn back the concerted and pervasive drive toward welfare repression that was taking place all across America in the mid-1970s.[67]

In December 1974, *Ramparts* published an ominous essay contributed by Terence McCarthy titled "An End to Affluence: The Last Christmas in America." Pundits, including McCarthy, noted that American citizens were as separated from the land as Europeans 200 years earlier; that America was entering an age of dearth and scarcity which would likely lead to class and inter-class conflict; and that the American Age of Affluence had officially ended March 1, 1973, when Europe compelled the dollar to float. Europe, McCarthy wrote, would no longer finance U.S. wars or the U.S.'s cost of living. "The U.S. was on its own," he explained.[68] The American people, he added, were as responsible

---

[67] Ibid, p. 26.

[68] Terence McCarthy, "An End to Affluence: The Last Christmas in America," *Ramparts Magazine*, December 1974, p. 52.

for the present and dire state of affairs as were the corporations that owned the American polity.

In other words, Americans got what they deserved for abandoning the revolution of the 1960s. The average American was, in short, complicit in the corporate-led counterrevolution of the 1970s. What was going to be required of the American people to turn the tide, McCarthy asserted, was acceptance of a social responsibility beyond anything before demanded of them. Every thinking man and woman, he argued, needed to undertake examination not only of what sort of America he or she wished to emerge from the present morass but of what was needed to be yielded so that the passage to the future would be as smooth as human effort could ensure. At base, he asserted, the fundamental requirement was recognition that the Affluent Society of yesterday, which was made possible by a rapacious economic system, deficit spending, and the largesse of European bankers, which was gone forever, and that the future would be what mankind made of it, within limits perhaps as constricting as those which America's forbears strove to escape in founding and building the country.[69]

In April 1975, *Ramparts* published another essay written by McCarthy titled "Tax Time: Soaking the Poor." In it he argued that the federal government was actively engaged in creating poverty by taking back by taxation what had not already been taken by inflation. He described a dehumanizing American system in which individuals and families were woefully exploited by being made into abstract "consumer units" as part of a system that was rigged to benefit the wealthy and corporations to the detriment of the poor and an ever-retracting American middleclass.

Ramparts, as the essays above illuminated, collectively depicted America as a land of incredible riches made possible by the systemic exploitation of the poorest Americans. While the 1960s seemed to some be a time of great promise

---

[69] Ibid, p. 75.

associated with the War on Poverty and the Great Society, those promises for a better and more equitable American system foundered on the shoals of the Vietnam War, a political conservative backlash to the gains made during the civil rights movement, and corporatization of the Supreme Court in the 1970s through the end of the twentieth century. The end of the twentieth century and early decades of the twenty-first century was a time in which poverty was increasingly blamed not on the architects and primary beneficiaries of the capitalist system, but rather increasingly blamed on capitalism's victims.

CHAPTER FIVE

"Scarcity in The Affluent Society"

In addition to chronicling the pervasive poverty that existed in the Affluent Society," many contributors to *Ramparts Magazine* highlighted the scarcity that existed throughout the United States during the 1960s and 1970s, which many perceived to be a moment in the nation's history when American power seemed to be increasingly challenged and waning by the reality that the empire was largely dependent on foreign oil supplies to power the nation's military might and Gross Domestic Product. The OPEC Oil embargo of 1973-74 in particular seemed to expose the American Empire's Achilles heel, which, many believed, created an existential crisis regarding the future of the militarized state.

Between October 1973 and April 1975 *Ramparts* published several essays about the energy crisis that the U.S. was suddenly forced to confront and which exposed the fact that if the emperor had clothes at all, they were woven by foreign oil men such as those associated with the Organization of the Petroleum Exporting Countries, an entity that had the potential to bring the American Empire to its knees by cutting off the military industrial complex's oil supply.

In October of 1973, in the midst of the OPEC embargo, *Ramparts* published an analysis titled "Out of Gas: Notes on the Energy Crisis," written by James Ridgeway, who was also the author of *The Last Play: The Struggle to Monopolize the World's Energy Resources* (1973). The "energy crisis," which was, Ridgeway explained, popularized by the major international oil corporations, worked on two levels: first, as natural resources became scarcer, they also became more expensive to extract, process, and market. The pressure had, Ridgeway continued, been building since the end of World War II, and consumers were finally becoming more painfully aware of it as they stood in long lines waiting to buy guy at their local service station. Assuming that the structure of the petroleum and mining industries remained the same, Ridgeway wrote, the inevitable result would be that fuel and energy prices would rise steadily. As that happened, the poorer segments of the American population would find it increasingly difficult to afford the energy that powered their homes and cars. Second, mineral resources were, Ridgeway noted, finite. As such, he explained, if the current rates of growth continued, they would be reduced substantially, and perhaps even exhausted by the end of the twentieth century, or more probably by the middle of the twenty-first century. Natural gas, then oil, would become even more scarce.

Even the supply of coal, which was considered to be abundant, could be exhausted rapidly if it was widely used as a base for synthetic gas. This situation was made confusing and rational solutions difficult by the existence of the energy industry, that conglomeration of large petroleum companies, which for the previous half-century had pretty much controlled the political and economic decisions affecting energy policies in the U.S. The business had traditionally been dominated by seven companies, the so-called "seven sisters," namely Standard Oil Company of New Jersey, Texaco, California Standard, Gulf, Mobil, Shell and British Petroleum, which collectively controlled two thirds of the world's oil, and dominated the refining, transportation and marketing of petroleum and natural gas products. Perhaps most importantly, the large petroleum companies were the only source of information the government had for the extent of the U.S.'s mineral fuels resources. They also dominated the technology for developing alternative fuels made from synthetics.

As such, Ridgeway argued, these large corporations ostensibly constituted a private government of energy. Any understanding of the "crisis" which these companies were so enthusiastically publicizing, Ridgeway declared, must begin with a brief history of oil operations in the decades preceding the 1970s. He then provided a history of the oil industry's lobbying and litigation activities that had led to up to the "crisis" of 1973. Corruption was, of course, central to that story. As bad as the OPEC embargo was for the American consumer, it was, Ridgeway argued, a boon for oil corporations because the short-term fuel oil and gasoline shortages were convenient vehicles for the major oil companies to tighten their grip on independents, and drive them out of business. The crisis was also a lever to force up the price of natural gas, and for a campaign to deregulate the price of gas, which would formally remove the federal government from regulation of fuel prices. More importantly, Ridgeway added, it would permit raising fuel prices to the point where oil companies could begin to seriously exploit synthetic gas made from coal, with enormous consequences for the nation's economy and ecology. Moreover, the nation did have serious energy problems, which it had to cope with in the waning decades of the twentieth century. The U.S.'s ability to handle them well, and with foresight, would, he concluded, likely hinge on the polity's ability to handle the major oil companies, to distinguish what was in their interest and what in fact served the needs of the population at large.[70]

In March 1974, *Ramparts* published a series of essays addressing the oil crisis. The first in the series was an essay written by Richard Parker titled "The Energy Crisis Is Coming...In About 200 Years." Despite the misleading title, Parker noted that the energy crisis was, in fact, an industry-wide crisis whose roots could be directly traced to 1969, which, he argued, was a monumental year that the petroleum industry wished "never happened" and was the worst year for the industry since Teapot Dome – a bribery scandal involving the administration of President Warren G. Harding (1921–1923) in which Secretary of the Interior Albert Bacon Fall had leased Navy petroleum reserves in Wyoming, and two locations in California, to

---

[70] James Ridgeway, "Out of Gas: Notes on the Energy Crisis," *Ramparts Magazine*, October 1973, p. 41.

private oil companies at low rates without competitive bidding. Convicted of accepting bribes from the oil companies, Fall became the first presidential cabinet member to go to prison; no one was convicted of paying the bribes.

So what happened in 1969 that appeared so dire for industry insiders? First, a Union Oil Platform blew open in the Santa Barbara Channel, spilling hundreds of thousands of barrels of oil, and causing an estimated $10-20 million in damage. The public outcry was so enormous, and came from so many quarters, including conservatives in Northern California, that Secretary of the Interior Wally Hickel, a Nixon appointee, placed a ban on future drilling, and, for a time, seemed to be considering the removal of existing off-shore rigs. Under increasing pressure from powerful senators such as Theodore Kennedy and Edmund Muskie, it became increasingly likely that Machiasport, Maine would be declared a "duty free" port, so that cheap Middle Eastern crude could slip by the oil import quotas to alleviate a shortage of heating oil in the New England area. Environmentalists, angered by the Santa Barbara oil spill, launched a series of massive suits designed to halt construction of the 800-mile Trans-Alaska Pipeline until oil companies could guarantee there would be no more ecological disasters. The Federal Trade Commission, ordering Standard Oil to cease-and-desist its promotion of "F-310" additive as "false and misleading," hinted that this was the beginning of an industry-wide investigation of advertising practices.

Then, in what proved to be crowning blows, first the Presidential committee studying oil import quotas, recommended their removal, and then Congress, in an attack upon "Oil's Holiest of Holies," concluded four decades of debate, by cutting the oil depletion allowance from 27.5 percent to 22 percent. "To the industry," Parker wrote, "the days of Teapot Dome must have looked, by comparison, almost idyllic." Despite hand-wringing by industry insiders, 1969 was, in fact, Parker explained, a wonderful year for petrol corporations around the world. World demand for petroleum was at an all-time high, and rising. U.S. energy needs alone had more than doubled in the previous twenty years, and the role of petroleum had steadily increased, together with natural gas supplying seventy percent of domestic energy requirements by 1965. Add to that the demands of Western Europe and Japan, whose own energy needs had risen even faster (and who lacked America's domestic supplies), and the picture for oil was "very bright indeed." [71]

Like Ridgeway, Parker argued that the "crisis" was, in fact, a boon for OPEC. It was likewise a boon for the Energy Cartel (Gulf, Texaco, Mobil, Standard of California, and Exxon), which collectively contributed $4,981,840 to Nixon's 1972 reelection campaign.[72] The "crisis," which Parker referred to as the "greatest

---

[71] Richard Parker, "The Energy Crisis Is Coming...In About 200 Years," *Ramparts Magazine*, March 1974, p. 30.

[72] Ibid, p. 43.

hoax of the century" (and far worse than the Teapot Dome scandal), was also a boon for banks such as Chase Manhattan, which was a major stockholder in Exxon. "Like it or not, Parker noted, Americans were victims of a great heist and most likely to go on paying for gas at fifty, sixty, seventy cents a gallon. "But someday," he concluded, "way down the long-distant horizon, when a real, honest-to-god, industry-destroying, economy-killing energy crisis finally looms into view, people maybe will realize a simple axiom: in oil, power grows out of the barrel, and when power is held by a few, it will be used for a few."[73]

Ramparts did not merely diagnosis the underlying causes and effects of the "energy crisis," it also proscribed means with which to address it. In March of 1974, for example, the magazine published an article titled "Alternate Energy: Here Comes the Sun," written by Gene Marine, who was author of *America the Raped: The*

---

[73] Ibid, p. 59.

Engineering Mentality and the Devastation of a Continent (1970). Large corporations, Marine argued, desired for consumers to believe that they manufactured energy as "a cobbler manufactured shoes." But this was, Marine argued, simply not the case. Energy corporations, he explained, spent a small amount of effort either releasing energy or changing its form, but indeed expended a great deal of effort moving energy resources around and selling it. Since burning fossil fuels produced most electricity, most of the energy Americans used in 1974 came from petroleum, and there was only so much petroleum to go around. Marine, however, disagreed with the oil energy's characterization of energy being very finite. There was, he asserted, enough, at current rates of use, for the next two or three hundred years; but politics had temporarily brought about a shortage, real or contrived, to America, and thus quite suddenly alternative energy came into fashion.

Marine described popular alternatives to petroleum including Coal gasification, which was done above ground burning coal slowly under pressure to produce methane gas. Vladimir Lenin, he noted, had some success with it in Soviet Russia in 1920s. Marine, however, was no advocate of that particular method due to the strip mining that was incumbent in the process. Another popularly proposed alternative to petrol and methane was, Marine noted, geothermal power. By 1993, he wrote, America could have 400 million kilowatts of electrical energy generated in the U.S. by this one method. Not only that, he added, it was relatively "clean," and would be "cheap." Other alternatives Marine advocated were solar power and also tidal and wind power. Conceptually speaking, tidal and wind worked much like solar power did. Garbage was another proposed alternative source of energy, which Marine advocated. He, however, lamented that not much research had been done into garbage as fuel because it was such an unglamorous field. Even less glamorous was what he referred to as "shit power," a method that used anaerobic bacteria to produce methane.[74] By the twenty-first century wind and solar had become prominent sources of energy, especially in the western portion of the U.S., but others, especially shit and garbage power, remained in very limited use as a viable alternative to traditional nonrenewable resources such as petroleum, which remained the most prominent source of American energy.

In May of 1974, *Ramparts* published an essay titled "What the Country Needs Is...," written by Peter Barnes, who was the West Coast Editor of *New Republic Magazine*. His essay was published shortly after the Stevenson Bill was proposed by eight senators, most notably Adlai Stevenson, who argued that the oil shortage highlighted the need for a federal oil corporation — something like the Tennessee Valley Authority. Barnes was, however, skeptical that New Deal-like government initiatives and programs could be affective in 1970s America,

---

[74] Gene Marine, "Alternate Energy: Here Comes the Sun," *Ramparts Magazine*, March 1974, pp. 33-36.

which, he argued, was a very different nation than the one that existed in the 1930s, prior to the rise of America's postwar military industrial complex. Even the generally positive experience of the TVA, he wrote, showed that a giant state monopoly, which TVA was within its service area, could become unresponsive to people's concerns; TVA's' obsession with strip-mining, he pointed out, was as tenacious as any private utility's was. His skepticism was tempered with an optimism rooted in the understanding that the energy crisis was dire and needed to be addressed. A public energy corporation, he concluded, or a series of them, might be followed by competitive public enterprises in other critical areas such as autos, steel, aluminum, drugs, banking and insurance.[75] The possibilities were, he asserted, exciting; but given the track record of the past century, celebration, he conceded, seemed premature.

---

[75] Peter Barnes, "What the Country Needs Is..." *Ramparts Magazine*, May 1974, p. 11.

Barnes' essay was followed by an article written by economist Terence McCarthy titled "An Age of Scarcity: Oil Is Only the Beginning." McCarthy argued that rising oil prices would also likely have dire consequences in other industries. He described the American economic system for energy corporations as follows: pay as little as (backed by your government) you can force foreigners to accept for their raw materials; increase minerals output abroad in accordance with your own national needs; process other people's natural resources in your own country to enforce dependence upon you as a market and to accelerate your own growth; in collusion with your government—using tariffs, import restrictions, and currency manipulations—charge as much as you can compel the world to pay for your finished exports regardless of the extorted cheapness of your materials imports; price your materials-bearing products at whatever the traffic will bear in domestic markets, with prices rising to just below that point at which social disorder might be provoked but never below that at which price advances at least equal wage increases.[76]

The foundation of this corrupt system, McCarthy argued, was the world's minerals industry, which was far more peculiar than the mere extraction of ores, and coal, and petroleum, etc., from the earth. On a world scale, it was, he explained, a means by which capitalist cartels and trusts shifted, gallon by gallon or ton by ton, bits of one country to other countries. And as they sold off one country bit by bit, they used the proceeds to buy up leases on other countries mile by mile which they then sold off bit by bit until nothing was left behind but "holes in the ground, some narrow and deep, some broad and shallow — until all the Third World became 'West Virginia.'"[77] In other words, multinational corporations were the imperialists, and the average American was as much a colonial subject as were people living in Saigon.

---

[76] Terence McCarthy, "An Age of Scarcity: Oil Is Only the Beginning," *Ramparts Magazine*, May 1974, p. 28.

[77] Ibid, p. 28.

In July of 1974, *Ramparts* published an essay written by Tom Zeman titled "The U.S. Economy: One Modest Proposal." He traced the collapse of the American economy to John Maynard Keynes, whose fanciful notions of an infinitely expanding, infinitely wasteful economy which seemed so irresistibly triumphant during the Cold War had by 1974 revealed itself to be "completely untenable."[78] Zeman suggested that one way to address the energy crisis and cratering American economy of the early 1970s was to pass a bottle bill – a law that would require a minimum refundable deposit on beer, soft drink and other beverage containers in order to ensure a high rate of recycling or reuse.

Deposits on beverage containers were not, he explained, a new idea. The deposit-refund system was, he explained, created by the beverage industry as a means of guaranteeing the return of their glass bottles to be washed,

---

[78] Tom Zeman, "The U.S. Economy: One Modest Proposal," *Ramparts Magazine*, July 1974, p. 40.

refilled and resold. When a retailer bought beverages from a distributor, a deposit could be paid to the distributor for each can or bottle purchased. The consumer paid the deposit to the retailer when buying the beverage. When the consumer returned the empty beverage container to the retail store, to a redemption center, or to a reverse vending machine, the deposit was refunded. The retailer recouped the deposit from the distributor, plus an additional handling fee. The handling fee, which generally ranged from one to three cents per container, helped cover the cost of handling the containers. The costs to distributors and bottlers could thus be offset by the sale of scrap cans and bottles and by short-term investments made on the deposits that were collected from retailers. In addition to this income, distributors and bottlers could reap windfall profits on beverage containers that consumers failed to return for the refund. The Council for a Cleaner Environment said it would save the energy equivalent of all die electricity needed for more than nine million affluent

Americans for one year. Another group called Sensible Citizens Against Throwaways (SCAT) claimed that Americans wasted on throwaways the energy equivalent of more than five million gallons of gasoline a day.

Zeman, however, feared that such responsible long-range planning would inevitably be derailed by corporations such as Alcoa, Reynolds, and U.S. Steel, who, despite talk about long-range business planning, seemed to think that the road to profitability most likely resided in the short run, not in long-range concerns about shortages and the environment. It was, Zeman argued, a sign of the continuing influence of these interest groups that Congress, despite glaring evidence of crisis, continued to think in the short run, too.

The bottle bill actually, however, passed in a few sates, most notably Oregon. But, as sensible as it might have seemed to environmentalists such as Zeman, it did not catch on very widely. Anheuser-Busch, The

Coca-Cola Company, and Pepsi-Cola Company were among those who opposed bottle bill legislation, in some cases funding opposition for newly proposed bills. Most states that did enact bottle bills used retail stores for collection, and these grocery stores were required to provide space and staff to facilitate the deposit refunds without receiving compensation, which further diminished the popularity and viability of a nationwide bottle bill. The programs were, in essence, funded by the state claiming any unredeemed deposits, leading to the possibility that if the return rate approached a hundred percent, the program would go bankrupt. Though bottle bills never quite caught on very widely throughout the U.S., the proposals in the early 1970s were some of the first concerted efforts to enact recycling legislation, which had caught on in most parts of the nation by the end of the twentieth century.

The energy crisis of the early 1970s pertained not merely to the perceived scarcity of oil, but also to food. In September 1974, *Ramparts* published an essay written by Terence McCarthy titled "Feast or Famine: The Choices for Mankind." In it he argued that the famine in the Sahel Desert could and should be prevented. There was, he argued, nowhere in the world that needed to be a desert so long as the industrialized world were willing to take some humanitarian austerity measures in their owns lives in terms of patterns of consumption and items consumed (such as oil and plastic). The population ratio, he asserted, was not a natural function, but a function of "mankind's failure to employ constructively the reasoning power with which nature had endowed it." Famine could, in short, he argued, be a thing of the past if citizens of industrialized nations committed to modifying their habits of consumption. This could, he explained, be accomplished, but institutional as well as cultural obstacles would, he conceded, be difficult to overcome.

He noted the widespread and fraudulent price-gouging in all industries, including the meat industry, which dictated the price of most other prices of goods bought at the supermarkets. He argued that by minimizing meat in the diet was to effect social economy in the production and distribution of nourishment. The profit-making mode of gathering foods from the farmer and distributing it to the consumer was, he explained, a willful barrier to more rational use and development of food resources. If Americans lowered that barrier, the U.S. could, he asserted, convert its output of assimilable protein for human consumption by about seven times the protein derived from eating cattle. The choice for mankind, he wrote, thus became very clear: run the risk of the extinction that demographers predicted for humankind; or reshape human social institutions to facilitate, not prevent, the required changes in food consumption patterns and the irrigation of the world's deserts. "It falls to us," he concluded, "to choose between life and death as the future for mankind. We have the power. Do we have the will?"[79]

McCarthy's essay was followed in the September 1974 edition of *Ramparts* by another article written by Zeman titled "Waste Not, Want Not: A Subversive Program for Energy in America." Zeman pointed out the irony that the energy industrialists that for so long had advertised themselves as the custodians of civilization were by the end of 1974 warning of the dire prospect of civilization collapsing if resources were expended. This apocalypticism, Zeman argued, was designed to further privatize American oil reserves and give corporations greater power and leverage to dictate prices based on the idea that demand was especially high concomitant to resources being very limited. His article offered some dire predictions about the future if Americans did not break what he referred to as their "addiction to energy

---

[79] Terence McCarthy, "Feast of Famine: The Choices For Mankind," *Ramparts Magazine*, September 1974, p. 32.

consumption." He advocated for everyone to dutifully turn lights off when not at home, employing alternative sources of energy such as wind and solar power, composting, and relying less on the television for pleasure and some household appliances such as dishwashers for quick convenience.[80]

In April 1975 *Ramparts* published another article written by Zeman titled "Solar Power Now." In it he argued that the obvious alternative to the fossil fuel and nuclear "nightmares" was to cut across the long, complicated process of photosynthesis, fossilization, extraction, combustion, and all the intermediate steps, and simply utilize the sun's free and plentiful energy directly. The problem was, he explained, learning how to concentrate and store it in a manner comparable to fossil fuels. As the energy industries were, he noted, quick to point out, large-scale, centralized

---

[80] Tom Zeman, "Waste Not, Want Not: A Subversive Program for Energy in America," *Ramparts Magazine*, September 1974, p. 33.

production of solar-generated electricity was not yet feasible.

But that was not, he bemused, really the point. "We could use solar energy now," he wrote, using decentralized solar collection equipment-in houses, apartment buildings, farms, offices, even factories — to cut deeply into the supplies of fossil fuel and electricity the energy industries provided in order to gradually wean "energy addicts" off of nonrenewable sources of energy and power. The most promising way of doing this in the long run was, he explained, the "photovoltaic cell," which converted sunlight into electrical energy. The cells worked, he wrote, they were used on orbiting satellites to provide electrical energy. Bringing down the cost of solar cells, to meet the whole spectrum of energy needs, would, he believed, constitute a major revolution in energy technology. It thus, he concluded, ought to be the nation's primary research and development commitment, far ahead of new weapons systems, nuclear reactors, and the like. Instead, he lamented, solar cell technology would receive about as much money in the foreseeable future as the nuclear reactor program spent in just a single day.[81]

In July of 1975, *Ramparts* published a three-part series of essays titled "Food – The Denial of Abundance. The first essay, "The Marketplace of Hunger," was contributed by Susan DeMarco and Susan Sechler, who were co-directors of the Agribusiness Accountability Project. They argued that food scarcity was not just man-made, but largely the result of Americans corporations. They noted that the United Nations estimated that in 1975 malnutrition affected about 460 million people, almost half of whom were children. Less conservative estimates put the figure closer to a billion. Over-all, the shortfalls in 1972 alone, DeMarco and Sechler explained, pushed the developing countries back to the per capita food

---

[81] Tom Zeman, "Solar Power Now," *Ramparts Magazine*, April 1975, p. 24.

production level they had reached a decade earlier. For those countries affected by the food crisis, the problems were twofold: first, international markets did not distribute sufficient quantities of food to meet even the minimum requirements of life, much less equity; secondly, after almost a quarter of a century of international "concern" about economic growth and development of poorer countries, their situation had continued to stagnate and even deteriorate between 1972 – 1975, to the point where not even the most basic need – food – could be met.

The U.S. was, the essayists noted, not only the largest exporter of food, accounting for nearly half the grain that moved into world markets, but it was also one of the largest importers of food. Together with other developed countries, the U.S. imported more protein from the developing countries than it collectively exported to them. The U.S. was also the leading innovator in the field of agricultural technology, and many countries (including the poor ones) looked to the U.S. as a model of how to make an agricultural system "work." American corporations were also the leaders in the numerous markets, which had been spawned by technology such as farm machinery, fertilizers, seeds, pesticides and other kinds of food production equipment. As a result, American solutions to agricultural production problems dominated thinking around the world.

In U.S. alone, DeMarco and Sechler wrote, the polity dealt with the poor and hungry through special programs such as food stamps or welfare, rather than attempting to build an economy which included them as full, working participants.[82] DeMarco and Sechler further noted that there was surplus in the U.S., both of money and food, to "solve" the problem of the poor without disturbing the economic system's basic operations or correcting its inevitable inequities. Projected internationally, to the

---

[82] Susan DeMarco and Susan Sechler, "The Marketplace of Hunger," *Ramparts Magazine*, July 1975, p. 34.

hundreds of millions of people who went hungry day after day and who were desperate for work, this approach – essentially one in which the rich could have and waste all they wished with enough left over to keep the poor alive – could not last because it simply did not work or make any ethical sense. The solution to the world hunger problem, DeMarco and Sechler explained, was within human control, but without the full cooperation of the U.S., through programs designed specifically to deal with the world hunger problem and through regular U.S. marketing activities, it was, they concluded, unlikely that a solution would be found until the "rich were willing to make sacrifices to ease the suffering for the rest of humanity."[83]

The third essay in "Food – The Denial of Abundance" published in the July 1975 edition of *Ramparts* was titled "A Declaration of Interdependence," written by Robert McAfee Brown, who was a professor of religious studies

---

[83] Ibid, p. 37.

at Stanford University. He argued that Nixon's attempt to sell the American people on the necessity for American "independence" by 1980 equated to America and Americans doing whatever was necessary to maintain, undiminished, the American way of life, no matter what happened elsewhere.

Such a vision was, Brown wrote, "both immoral and impossible."[84] Even if it could be achieved, he surmised, it would be immoral to assume that a few wealthy Americans had the right to all they wanted while the rest perished, populating a lavish oasis in an "ever-widening desert of want and destitution." Much of the discussion about food scarcity, he explained, centered on what was called "lifeboat ethics" in which the rich nations had their own lifeboats, full up but seaworthy, while the poor nations were in badly provisioned boats that were sinking. The poor in this victim-blaming scenario

---

[84] Robert McAfee Brown, "A Declaration of Interdependence," *Ramparts Magazine*, July 1975, p. 43.

were, he explained, trying to climb into the lifeboats of the rich. The rich, so the theory went, were thus justified in drowning the poor, because if the poor were able to claw their way on board the rich lifeboats, they would soon run short of provisions and be swamped, and everybody would perish.

Brown provided a counter-image of the rich in a luxury liner or yacht rather than lifeboats, and that there was actually plenty of food and space on board, so that the rich, even if they decided to keep the first-class section of the vessel to themselves, could afford to let the poor on board. But there was, he elaborated, an even more accurate image, the image of earth as a spaceship. The value of thinking of the earth as a spaceship, he asserted, was that it stressed the element of interdependence. He thus rhetorically asked readers: "How are the resources aboard this spaceship being divided?"[85]

---

[85] Ibid, p. 44.

Instead of 3.6 billion people, he insisted, think of a crew of five persons, each representing a segment of humanity. The Judeo-Christian, white Western, affluent, of the five crew members had the use of eighty percent of the available life resources and amenities aboard the spacecraft. The other four crew members had to split the other twenty percent amongst themselves. He argued that the one crew member with eighty percent of the resources was either setting himself up for mutiny, or if he were to outlive the other crew members due to his superabundance of resources, the spacecraft (earth) would not long survive his eventual death as a rich man with no one to even compare his wealth to. Here was a case where a moral concern would, Brown argued, inevitably coincide with the realistic self-interest of the entire human family. And since nations did not usually act for moral or altruistic reasons, but out of a sense of national self-interest, he concluded, there was at least a small chance that the rich nations might one day realize that they were in fact pursuing their own destruction and inevitable demise.

It is a bit eye-opening to read articles predicting the complete collapse of humanity as a result of scarcity considering most history books focus so heavily on the rise of the Affluent Society in the decades after World War II and give such short-shrift to the energy crisis and famine that was, at least to *Ramparts*, an incredibly pressing issue and moment in world history. Though there was by the turn of the twenty-first century a great deal of concern regarding global warming amongst some politicians like Al Gore, who won a Nobel Prize in part for his part in the production of the documentary film, *An Inconvenient Truth* (2006), there had been no great endeavor spearheaded by the American government to address the damage done to the planet as a result of nonrenewable resources largely due to the fact that oil, gas, and coal producing and refining corporations have as much power and influence over the polity in the twenty-first century as they did during the 1960s and 1970s. In many cases, the gains won by environmentalists were rolled back, especially during the administration of President Donald Trump, a corporatist who put industry insiders in charge of organizations such as the Environmental Protection Agency. The Trump administration most notably lowered the standards of fuel emissions for automobile companies, which was a blow to those hoping to significantly address the global warming crisis.

CHAPTER SIX

"Miseducating an Empire"

Ramparts Magazine published several stories about corruption in the realm of American education, which the publication tended to depict as being increasingly infiltrated by special interest groups, the Central Intelligence Agency, and corporations associated with the military industrial complex. The first such essay was published in March 1965. It was an editorial titled "The Lesson of Berkeley" that described the Free Speech Movement as a singularly important event in American history. The Free Speech Movement began as a student protest took place during the 1964–1965 academic year on the campus of the University of California, Berkeley. The informal leadership of students included Mario Savio, Brian Turner, Bettina Aptheker, Steve Weissman, and Jackie and Art Goldberg (the latter of whom later became an editor at *Ramparts Magazine*).

In protests unprecedented in scope at the time, students insisted that the university administration lift the ban of on-campus political activities and acknowledge the students' right to free speech and academic freedom. "American university life," the editors wrote, "will never be the same after the student rebellion—a rebellion supported by the faculty— against a paternalistic and bungling administration that was incapable of recognizing that students could actually be serious about such abstract constitutional issues as free political movement and free speech."[86] Cal Berkeley President Clark Kerr's administration, the editors noted, offered no substantial explanation for the restrictions of students' basic constitutional rights. The students at Berkeley, the editors added, assumed that Kerr was responding to pressure from businessmen in surrounding communities who were disturbed at the involvement of UC students in civil rights demonstrations.

---

[86] *Ramparts* editorial staff, "The Lesson of Berkeley," *Ramparts Magazine*, March 1965, p. 3.

The impasse was never resolved. It culminated in the arrest of nearly eight-hundred students in a massive sit-in demonstration in Sproul Hall, the university administration building, in December 1964. "The attitude of the administration," the editors wrote, "made such an unseemly event possible."[87] These students did not, the editors explained, feed on abstract political theory; they were courageously battling against the traditional bureaucratic and established methods because they saw those methods as failing, critically, to solve the great moral issues facing this nation: racial justice, the existence of poverty in the midst of plenty, the establishment of peace in a world dominated by the thermonuclear threat. The students were asking the UC administration to raze the ivory towers, to give them freedom to struggle with the difficult problems of the world outside the campus. There was, the editors presciently declared, no doubt that, after the events December 1964, students in other colleges would

---

[87] Ibid, p. 3.

put this question to their own administrations. And unless college administrators understood what Clark Kerr did not, the editors concluded, they might be faced with another Berkeley, which was the lesson to be learned.

Ramparts published also several stories about the CIA that depicted the organization as a corrupt and amoral imperial force determined to maintain the economic and political status quo that existed prior to the World Wars. In April 1966, for example, the editors of *Ramparts* published an essay titled "MSU: The University on the Make," written by Warren Hinckle in conjunction with research editor Sol Stern, and a foreign relations editor named Robert Scheer. Material appearing in this special report originated in Scheer's pamphlet, "How the U.S. Got Involved in Vietnam." The editors' essay underscored the extent to which militarization had come to shape hallowed American cultural institutions, including higher education.

The "decay in academic principles" of higher education, the editors wrote, could be traced to Harold Stassen and Clark Kerr, but President John A. Hannah of Michigan State University "best exemplified it."[88] Stassen, of the International Cooperation Administration, was, Hinckle wrote, responsible for the concept that American universities should be tapped as "manpower reservoirs" for the extension of Americanism abroad, and Clark Kerr, "the embattled Berkeley savant," first came up with the vision of the large university as a "service station" to society. Hannah, who Hinckle described as an "Eisenhower liberal" with a penchant for public service, had made these high-minded concepts the raison d'être of MSU. He had, nonetheless, permitted CIA agents to hide within the ranks of MSU professors. All of these agents, Hinckle added, were listed as members of the MSU Project staff and were

---

[88] Warren Hinckle, Sol Stern, and Robert Scheer, "MSU: The University on the Make," *Ramparts Magazine*, April 1966, p. 13.

formally appointed by the University Board of Trustees. Several of the agents were given academic rank and were paid by the University Project.

The agents' mission at MSU was to engage in counterespionage and counterintelligence. Their "cover" was within the police administration division of the Michigan State Group. The CIA unit was self-contained, and appeared on an official organization chart of the MSU Project as "VBI (the South Vietnamese version of the FBI): INTERNAL SECURITY SECTION." This five-man team was the largest section within the police administration division of the MSU Vietnam operation. The police administration division in turn was by far the largest of the three divisions of the MSU Group.

In 1955 South Vietnamese President Ngo Diem's Army, which was paid for entirely by the U.S. government, wiped out the Saigon Police force, which, he feared, were not completely loyal to him. The gargantuan task of rebuilding the entire Vietnam police apparatus, from traffic cop to interrogation expert, as a loyal agent of the Diem government then fell to Michigan State University. Diem, lacking popular support in his own nation, could only retain power through an effective police and security network propped up by the U.S.

The American embassy, Hinckle explained, urgently signaled the MSU contingent to concentrate on this problem, and, "like good team players from a school with a proud football tradition, the professors went along." For six years, MSU professors advised Diem on how to dispose of potential enemies. MSU in East Lansing, Hinckle wrote, also seemed to become a police state during the six years MSU professors masterminded the assassination of Diem's (real and imagined) enemies. There was the campus police — a complement of roughly thirty-five men in blue uniforms; there were the professors and visiting firemen at the School of Police Administration; and the state police headquarters adjoined MSU. But they did not seem to make Hannah, who feared a "Berkeley-style" revolt at MSU, feel very safe.

Hannah, who was, Hinckle wrote, "ever weary of outside agitators," had suggested that there was an "apparatus" at work on campus that was a "tool for international communism." MSU police thus had a special detail charged with keeping tabs on student political activities, especially anything "radical" in nature. Hannah's concern over Berkeley was, Hinckle explained, "more than apocryphal." If the Berkeley experience meant any one thing to Hannah," Hinckle added, it meant that the University was not doing its job. It had lost its sense of purpose; it no longer had meaning to the students. In that sense, East Lansing was, Hinckle assured readers, another Berkeley. The essential query, which must be asked before the discussion of Michigan State's behavior thus, Hinckle concluded, could be put into any rational perspective: "what the hell is a university doing buying guns, anyway?"[89]

In August 1966, *Ramparts* implicated the Ivy League in war profiteering in an article titled "War Catalogue of Penn University," written by Sol Stern. Penn, Stern wrote, entertained "bizarre and compromising relationships" with the U.S. military establishment.[90] The school's connections were, Stern added, typical of the large university, which had to come to terms with an environment in which Cold War priorities shaped educational policies. At Penn, Stern wrote, the price of accommodation had been high both in intellectual independence and academic integrity. It spawned the most important university center for germ and chemical warfare research in the country — research that was being applied directly in

---

[89] Ibid, p. 22.

[90] Sol Stern, "War Catalogue of Penn University," *Ramparts Magazine*, August 1966, p. 31.

Vietnam to destroy the food crops of civilian populations.

The University also, Stern noted, offered a political science course, which served no other function than to train future CIA agents. Penn's relationship with the U.S. military was, Stern explained, the result not of philosophical commitments but of dependence. Penn was not so much a university on the make as MSU was described to be by Hinckle. Penn was kept solvent by federal contracts that it would have had difficulty operating as major university in a major metropolitan area (Philadelphia, Pennsylvania) had the school had to forego Defense Department financing. Government grants provided the largest single source of the University's total income—approximately $25 million out of a university budget of almost $90 million.[91]

Penn, despite its official membership in the Ivy League, did not have, as Stern described

_____

[91] Ibid, p. 31.

them, "the well-heeled or loyal" alumni of a Princeton, Yale or a Harvard. And as a private university, its support from the state government was minimal. To keep the books balanced, the University president had to become what Stern referred to as "a wheeler-dealer" among foundations, the state legislature, and alumni. But only the federal government provided a reliable and steady source of financial support for Penn. Portions of this support came in classified contracts with the Defense Department, which forced the University to give up many of its traditional prerogatives of open and free research. Well-endowed institutions such as Harvard could, Stern concluded, reject such secret contracts. But for Penn, with its precarious financial status, principle had become a luxury it could no longer afford.

In March 1967, *Ramparts* published an essay written by Adam Hochschild titled "The Death of a President," which chronicled the rise and fall of Clark Kerr. Kerr helped build one of the biggest and best endowed university systems in the state of California that the world had ever known. But his tenure was marred in 1964 when Berkeley students led the Free Speech Movement in protest of regulations limiting political activities on campus, including civil rights advocacy and also protests against the Vietnam War. The protests culminated in hundreds of students being arrested.

Kerr's initial decision was to not expel Cal students that participated in sit-ins. That decision evolved into reluctance to expel students who later would protest on campus in a series of escalating events on the Berkeley campus in late 1964. Kerr was criticized both by students for not agreeing to their demands and by conservative UC Regent Edwin Pauley and others for responding what many perceived to be too leniently to student unrest.

Pauley approached CIA Director John McCone (a Berkeley alum and associate) for assistance. McCone in turn met with FBI Director J. Edgar Hoover, who agreed to supply Pauley with confidential FBI information on "ultra-liberal" regents, faculty members, and students, and to assist in removing Kerr. The FBI assisted Pauley and Ronald Reagan in portraying Kerr as a dangerous leftist, which contributed to Kerr's dismissal, though he was by no means a fellow traveler. Not only did Kerr become, Hochschild wrote, "a martyr for the age where compromise in the multiversity was possible," his dismissal was also "a symbol of the passing of the secure Cold War period of national consensus."[92]

Also in March 1967, *Ramparts* published an article titled "NSA and the CIA" written by Sol Stern about the secrecy of the CIA and NSA funding or infiltrating student organizations. The NSA in this context is not a reference to the National Security Agency. NSA in 1967 referred to the National Student Organization, a confederation of college and university student governments that was in operation from 1947 to

---

[92] Adam Hochschild, "The Death of a President," *Ramparts Magazine*, March 1967, p. 28.

1978 with, Stern wrote, international programs in the "best tradition of cultural exchanges between countries."[93] Stern's essay expressed lament that the CIA had funded and infiltrated the organization in an attempt to garner information that might undermine liberal causes. "The twisted sickness of this Orwellian argument should speak for itself," Stern wrote. Like the editorial staff in 1966, Stern believed the insidious infiltration of higher education, including the NSA, to be evidence of how far removed from Enlightened ideas of genuine liberty, equality, and justice the United States had drifted in the interest of consolidating its imperial power. The CIA's influence in the NSA, Stern argued, also indicated "how deeply the corruption of means for ends" had "become ingrained" in American society by the 1960s, "and how much dishonesty" was "tolerated in the name of the Cold War."[94]

[93] Sol Stern, "NSA and the CIA," *Ramparts Magazine*, March 1967, p. 38.

[94] Ibid, p. 38.

In April 1967, *Ramparts* published an editorial titled "How the CIA Turns Foreign Students Into Traitors." The essayists examined the CIA's clandestine funding of student groups, most particularly the American Friends of the Middle East. The bulk of the CIA's largesse came from five foundations identified as CIA fronts: the San Jacinto Foundation of Houston, the Chesapeake Foundation of Baltimore, the Andrew Hamilton Fund of Philadelphia, the Broad-High Foundation of Columbus, and the Granary Fund of Boston.

In addition to holding the purse strings of AFME, the CIA also, the editors explained, installed operatives on the staff, including director Kermit Roosevelt, the CIA agent who engineered the overthrow of Premier Mossadegh of Iran in 1953. Much of the CIA's money went to the AFME department of student affairs. Through this branch, AFME worked with other American educational organizations, like the prestigious Institute of International Education,

---

and with official government agencies, in bringing foreign students to the U.S. AFME's department of student affairs also meddled in the politics of the foreign student organizations in the U.S., using its CIA money to pay the bills of these organizations and as bait for them to take the "correct" political line. The CIA, in short, secretly used public funds to co-opt and subvert independent American student organizations. "It is that much more abominable when foreign students," the editors concluded, "lured into this country by the promise of honesty, are bribed and corrupted, and turned into traitors against their own societies."[95]

Seemingly following up on Stern's article about the CIA infiltrating the National Student Organization published in the March 1967 edition of *Ramparts* and the CIA's subsequent influence on student organizations around the globe such as American Friends of the Middle East, the editors published a short essay in

---

[95] Ibid, p. 24.

September 1967 titled "The CIA: Festivals and Finks," written by John Spitzer. He used an upcoming student conference in Ljubljana, Yugoslavia (scheduled for August 1968), which was to be cosponsored by the German Students for a Democratic Society, as evidence of how drastically student organizations such as SDS seemed to have radicalized by 1967, especially in contrast to the student groups such as NSA, which were fronts for CIA activity. The Yugoslavian conference was entitled "Anti-imperialist, anti-capitalist struggles and student revolts: analysis and strategy," which the editors contrasted with the World Youth Festival, known as Solidarity, Peace, and Friendship Convention. Spitzer sardonically noted that "neither the Social Democrats nor the CIA" were invited to the Yugoslavian conference.[96]

The theme of the military industrial complex subsuming all spheres of American

---

[96] John Spitzer, "The CIA: *Festivals and Finks*," *Ramparts Magazine*, September 7, 1967, p. 14.

society continued in February 1968 edition of *Ramparts*, which published an essay titled "The Man Who Came in From the Cold (War)," written by Marcus G. Raskin. The essay focused on Charles Hitch, who, in 1968, became President of the University of California at Berkeley, which was the largest and most well-developed university system in the world. Before becoming President of California's university system, Hitch had been the Comptroller of the Department of Defense, a senior staff economist of the RAND Corporation, an advisor on the use and acquisition of military power, and, as Raskin described him, "a war planner/maker extraordinary."

Hitch also worked in the Office of Strategic Affairs (The OSS), the forerunner to the CIA, during World War II, helping develop operations research. After World War II, Hitch went to the RAND Corporation, where he worked on military and war problems, starting from the assumption that military problems were essentially economic problems because they had to do with determining how to allocate resources in the most efficient way. As a result of his work at RAND and his promulgation of the technique of planning, programming and budgeting, he became the comptroller of the Department of Defense, "the money manager."

He later became vice-president of the University of California, basically in charge of finance management for the University. Although these jobs might appear dull, they were, Raskin explained, basic to shaping the structure of the American national security system in the decades after World War II, and hence the contours of American society writ large. Hitch was chosen, Raskin stated, because in the minds of the Board of Regents he seemed to be noncontroversial—concerned mostly with figures, budgets and future campus planning. He had the proper academic credentials, and his quiet, conservative demeanor would fit in nicely with a state legislature and conservative governor (Ronald Reagan) who were antipathetic to the university faculty and students. The liberals on the Board of Regents also, Raskin believed, thought Hitch was a good choice because the universities were going to be decentralized when the Byrne Report, calling for autonomy of each of the state universities, was implemented.

No doubt, Raskin noted, the Regents must also have had reasoned that Hitch would be able to obtain grants from the Department of Defense and other areas of the federal establishment at a time when such federal grants were becoming scarcer and harder to obtain and the possibility of cutbacks by the California State legislature was very great. Hitch would, Raskin predicted, follow the idea of centralized budgetary control for all the universities in much the same way he had acted for the secretary of Defense in controlling the purse strings of the individual military services. Hitch and his staff, using their budgetary technique as the control mechanism, and posing as disinterested analysts, would, Raskin asserted, set the policy and direction of the state universities in California.

Raskin also referred to Hitch as one of many "Megadeath Intellectuals" who had matriculated from the state department to the university system and who peddled "nonsense and madness."[97] Raskin expressed belief that Hitch and other "Megadeath Intellectuals'" work was similar to the work of advertising agents on Madison Avenue who huckstered products. Raskin was thus especially disturbed that Hitch had ended up as president of the University of California. The Berkeley revolt of 1964, Raskin asserted, had to be considered in the light of the appointment of Hitch. While students called for democracy and constitutional controls, Raskin noted, Hitch helped build, unify and strengthen a military/industrial class which would not be accountable except to the militarized civilian — men like himself who never realized that the entire national security system as it came to be conceived was "rotten to the core." This system, Raskin argued, "made hostages of whole

---

[97] Marcus G. Raskin, "The Man Who Came in From the Cold (War)," *Ramparts Magazine*, February 1968, p. 34.

societies for the views of a few." Concerned about process and function but not assumptions and consequences, men like Hitch had, Raskin lamented, helped distort priorities in American life and judgment in American statecraft. It was thus, Raskin wrote, a "tragedy of the American present that neither the content nor the consequences of the work of such men seem to be counted against them."

Perhaps, Raskin hoped, Hitch would set up new universities in California which would address themselves to the modern economic and political question of how the total world resources could be used for the benefit of all of mankind, rather than the rich few. Unfortunately, Raskin wrote, it was far more likely that Hitch would "act as an advisor to Governor Reagan on how to keep the university community in line and that he would try to bring the governor closer to understanding the modern war-maker's defense ideology." President Hitch would, Raskin noted, also be valuable in bringing the governor and the state university system closer to the nationally oriented defense corporations on the west coast. Raskin concluded by assailing the Board of Regents and Governor Reagan for forcing the university into a role "subservient to state power," which, he believed, merely ensured the "decline of the university as the keeper of the values of universal humanism, and the decline of American civilization."[98]

In June 1968, *Ramparts* published an exclusive report titled "Columbia," which was written by the editorial staff at the magazine with the assistance of staff reporters from *The Liberation News Service* in New York City. The report chronicled a long relationship between Columbia University and American corporations such as Dow Chemical. From 1900 – 1968, Columbia was, the editors explained, systemically taken over by corporations via friendly relations with three university presidents, the most recent of which was John

---

[98] Ibid, p. 34.

Lindsay, the Mayor of New York City from 1959 – 1965.

Grayson Kirk, the president of the university at the time the editorial was published in *Ramparts*, was presented by the editors to be as much of a strawman of the New Left as Clark Kerr was in contrast to Mario Savio in Berkeley in 1964. Kirk had banned student demonstrations in campus building prior to the 1968 student occupation of campus buildings. The ban even prevented students from collecting signatures for petitions inside campus buildings. The editors thus described Columbia's campus to be a "growing police state" concomitant to the American police becoming more militarized in reaction to the antiwar movement.

The editors then elaborated that in the "Employment Opportunities" booklet for graduates of Columbia's School of International Affairs, which was originally printed in 1960, the CIA was described as the preferred career opportunity for graduates — ahead of the State Department, the Foreign Service, the USIA and the United Nations, which was near the bottom of Columbia's list of desirable jobs for recent graduates. The importance of the Columbia upheaval in 1968, the editors explained, was not in any concrete institutional changes that might eventually be achieved on that campus, although such a resolution was, they conceded, obviously important for the students and faculty who took part, but rather in its "total educational impact."

The Columbia uprising, the editors pointed out, had further polarized people on both ends of the American political spectrum. The editors, however, saw this as a positive turn of events since "the old reasonableness" was "no more than a cover, permitting education to be a vacuous thing" that was increasingly "meaningless in people's lives."[99] The editors thus described professors who worked on germ warfare next to others who spent their time doing humanistic research as a "crisis" that

---

[99] *Ramparts'* editorial staff, "Columbia: An Exclusive Report," *Ramparts Magazine*, June 15, 1968, p. 39.

demanded swift redress. The university was, the editors explained, especially divided into camps, each of which was stimulated to try to make its knowledge and its view of the world more meaningful. All of this was, they argued, "purgative" and ultimately "much healthier than the false sense of routine and reason," which served to obscure an enormous amount of banality of evil that existed throughout Cold War American society and which corrupted the mission of higher education.

As such, the editors asserted, by disrupting the orderly process "the veil had been lifted; the institution had been observed to have real interests, and one could determine for oneself whether he or she wished to support those interests." The editors added that since the end of World War II, American students had "blithely accepted the advice of their teachers and made appropriate adjustments to a suffocating society." Their professors, of course, had "surrendered first;" many of them were ex-radicals and reformers who had "given up the dream of radical change in order to celebrate the society because it was successful in delivering material goods." All of this was done in the name of "realism" and "scientific objectivity" and was especially championed by Columbia professor of sociology Daniel Bell as the "End of Ideology," a phrase that for the radical students became an epitaph for an age. Against the Daniel Bells and the David Trumans the radical Columbia students were, the editors asserted, unashamedly old-fashioned enough to offer up a utopian vision of social institutions that did not need to defend their values by repression. The students made the "great refusal; they were romantic; they dreamed the impossible." Those among their professors who could think in a radical way, the editors concluded, "inevitably became apologists for the existing order under the guise of merely describing it, in the vernacular: That's the way it is—you can't change it." Against such "realism," the members of Columbia's short-lived new society rebelled, in the vernacular: "Up against the wall, motherfuckers!"[100]

In December 1968, *Ramparts* published an essay titled "School's Out," contributed by Gene Marine and Reese Erlich. They quoted Max Rafferty, who was the California State Superintendent of Public Instruction as saying, "If I were a college president we would have a lot fewer students, a lot fewer professors and a lot more order."[101] The essay chronicled the plight of Nesbit Crutchfield, who was a student at San Francisco State College and a member of the Black Students Union. Nesbit and other protesters had been attacked by unprovoked police officers. One of the offending officers jammed his knee into Crutchfield's back while the other clubbed him with a baton. When the police officers got up, Crutchfield could not, so they dragged him away. Nesbit was then charged with assaulting a police officer. Seven

---

[100] Ibid, p. 39.
[101] Gene Marine and Reese Erlich, "School's Out," *Ramparts Magazine*, December 14, 1968, p. 17.

students and a faculty member were also arrested for assault and related charges along with Nesbit. Within an hour, a once apathetic crowd of students had turned into an angry and united group—and at one point, near the education building, nearly eight-hundred students stood facing a dozen frightened police officers.

Like that, San Francisco State College had become embroiled in one of the most successful student strikes since the 1930s—and African Americans led it. Supported by whites and other minority students, the black movement leaders, such as Crutchfield, were determined to define for themselves the nature of their college education. They demanded to learn, Marine and Erlich wrote, skills that they could bring back to the ghettos of the Fillmore and Hunter's Point. Put simply, Marine and Erlich added, the African American student-activists wanted San Francisco State to serve the people of their neighborhoods—not the corporations that controlled those communities.

For the black and Third World students on campus, Marine and Erlich explained, the issue was clear from the beginning: the right of self-determination for themselves and their communities. This attempt to turn mass education into something which was truly for the masses was, the essayists asserted, an effort that the trustees of the state college system were "not about to tolerate;" but it was a demand that was going to arise in every one of the urban colleges across the country. "For this reason alone," they wrote, "the trouble at San Francisco State" stretched far beyond the outer fringes of San Francisco's commuter belt. Berkeley or Columbia, they concluded, "may be lingering in the background somewhere as ideals of campus radicalism, but even if you live in Kansas City, San Francisco State is close to home."[102]

In May 1969, *Ramparts* published an essay titled "Billion Dollar Brains: How Wealth Puts Knowledge in its Pocket," written by David

---

[102] Ibid, p. 17.

Horowitz, chronicled an academic revolution fostered with federal support that created the "sinews of a global empire." Higher education, which Horowitz argued was subservient to power, was "shaped by the ubiquitous charity of the foundations and the guiding mastery of wealth."[103] Horowitz described higher education as being made by and for America's capitalist class. He, as such, rhetorically wondered: Where would the radical ideas and groundbreaking research necessary to topple capitalism come from if not from the universities? He lamented that capitalism had seemed to irrevocably corrupted higher education to its core, which ensured that the social inequity at the root of capitalism would remain, unless the trend were somehow to be reversed.

In October 1969, *Ramparts* published another essay written by Horowitz titled "Sinews of Empire." In it he lamented just how far

---

[103] David Horowitz, "Billion Dollar Brains: How Wealth Puts Knowledge in its Pocket," *Ramparts Magazine*, May 1969, p. 36.

academia had fallen from the ideal of open, critical, independent scholarship. The universities, Horowitz explained, were once thought to constitute a vital, independent, countervailing estate, but the modern university had, he asserted, been converted into an Office of External Research for the State Department, the Pentagon, and international corporations. The postwar takeover of the university, Horowitz explained, was accomplished with "less finesse and reserve than a corporate conglomerate customarily showed a newly acquired subsidiary," and it was thus symbolic that the new management team that was to reorganize the university from "within" was in fact drawn largely from the unlikely and forbidding ranks of the American World War II intelligence arm, the Office of Strategic Services.[104]

Horowitz noted an expose *Ramparts* had published in April of 1966 about the role of the

---

[104] David Horowitz, "Sinews of Empire," *Ramparts Magazine*, October 1969, p. 33.

CIA at Michigan State University and professors actively aiding the American military's infiltration of Vietnamese universities in the interest of transforming students into spies. What may have seemed like an isolated scandal in 1966 could by 1969, Horowitz declared, be identified "as a universal condition of organized intellect in America." The saddest part, he believed, was that the academics had become such "eager victims." They had, he asserted, "internalized the limits placed upon them by the Cold War conformity" that had become endemic in American higher education in the decades after World War II. And though academics, Horowitz wrote, fiercely upheld strict academic professionalism, that professionalism was "no more than expert servitude to oppressive power," and to a system whose wages were "poverty and blood." They did not, Horowitz concluded, see that what they had really embraced was "the perverted professionalism of the mercenary and the hired gun."[105]

In July 1972, *Ramparts* published an essay titled "I.Q. Tests: Building Blocks for the New Class System," written by Noam Chomsky, who chronicled the controversial views of Harvard Psychologist Richard Herrnstein, whose ideas first received widespread attention when they were presented, under the laconic title "I.Q." in the September 1971 edition of *The Atlantic*. Hernstein and other respected scholars of the era, Chomsky explained, believed that the roots of the seemingly intractable racial conflict in the U.S. could best be explained by probing for a statistical margin of racial difference. Hernstein purported to show that American society was drifting inexorably towards a stable hereditary meritocracy, towards a social stratification determined by inborn differences and a

---

[105] Ibid, p. 42.

corresponding distribution of "rewards."[106] I.Q., in short, was, Hernstein asserted, likely heritable.

Chomsky noted that an advertisement in *The Harvard Crimson* (November 29, 1971), signed by many faculty members, referred to the "disturbing conclusion that 'intelligence' was largely genetic, so that over many, many years society might evolve into classes marked by distinctly different levels of ability."[107] Chomsky concluded the essay by rhetorically asking readers:

> Would it also be disturbing to discover that relative height, or musical talent, or rank in running the 100-yard dash, is in part genetically determined? Why should one have preconceptions one way or another about these questions, and how do the answers to them, whatever they may be, relate either to serious scientific issues (in

---

[106] Noam Chomsky, "I.Q. Tests: Building Blocks for the New Class System," *Ramparts Magazine*, July 1972, p. 26.

[107] Ibid, p. 30.

the present state of our knowledge) or to social practice, in a decent society?[108]

Chomsky, in other words, seemed determined to compel readers to examine the residue of Social Darwinism that continued to be deeply woven into the fabric of American academe.

In July 1972, *Ramparts* published an essay titled "The Open Schoolroom: New Worlds for Old Deceptions," written by Jonathan Kozol, who was the author of *Free Schools* (1972). Kozol, an educational reformer, noted that free schools were controlled by special interest groups such as the Carnegie Foundation, which wanted to inject utopianism into inner city schools. Kozol, however, noted how difficult even the best funded and staffed schools would be for children suffering poverty and the consequences of it, which might include hunger, dislocation, absentee parents, and lack of health care. The only forms of educational innovation that were "serious and worth consideration" in the U.S. in

---

[108] Ibid, p. 30.

the year of 1972 were, he asserted, those which constituted "direct rebellion, explicit confrontation or totally independent ventures".[109] This included independent strip mall-storefront type schools affiliated with local school districts that provided an alternative to mainstream public education in cases in which the curriculum was very conservative and/or outdated in terms of teaching children to think critically. In other words, Kozol was against the schools that had the effect of diminishing the potential for poor children to develop the ability to think critically about the nature of capitalism and its pernicious impact in American public life.

In August 1972, *Ramparts* published an essay titled "Classroom Surveillance by Kodak (12 years ahead of its time)," contributed by Buddy Nevins. His essay foreshadowed the rise of the security industrial complex in the U.S. He explained the cultural significance of the school

---

[109] Jonathan Kozol, "The Open Schoolroom: New Worlds for Old Deceptions," *Ramparts Magazine*, July 1972, p. 42.

board of Polk County, Florida, installing cameras so that administrators could monitor junior and senior high school students in the halls and while eating lunch. *Rolling Stone Magazine*, Nevins wrote, was also banned in Polk County schools. Nothing, however, had actually substantively changed in terms of student behavior or academic performance after the surveillance cameras had been installed in Polk County. In fact, Nevins explained, the only modification in the students' behavior was the amount of "subterfuge and fear." He quoted one student as saying that the school day was "like being in jail for six hours."[110] Nevins perceived surveillance cameras in schools, which by the second decade of the twenty-first century had become ubiquitous in the U.S., to be evidence of creeping Orwellianism in what seemed to be an the increasingly fascist and militarized surveillance

---

[110] Buddy Nevins, "Classroom Surveillance by Kodak (12 years ahead of its time)," *Ramparts Magazine*, August 1972, p. 6.

state prophesied by critical theorists such as Michel Foucault.

In March 1974, *Ramparts* published an essay titled "Good Morning Class, My Name is Bzzz Vzz Crackle," contributed by Michael Seltzer, who taught anthropology at the University of Wisconsin at Superior, and Howard Karger, who was an ex-member of the Teacher Corps. Their essay chronicled the takeover of Third World higher education by Corporate America. "The knowledge industry," the authors argued, had followed the "monopoly capital route" of the oil, steel and automotive industries. In other words, an initial phase of massive competition between many corporations had been replaced by a situation where the entire market was, by 1974, controlled by a handful of corporate giants including IBM, RCA, *Time-Life*, ATT, ITT, Singer and Xerox, entities that collectively "dominated the marketplace of knowledge."[111]

For the corporation, Seltzer and Karger argued, the Third World offered considerably more than just the immediate profits to be gleaned from a total takeover of educational institutions. If their global electronic classroom did become a reality, it would insure them a "receptive population passively awaiting their orders to produce, buy and die, if need be, for the cause of American profits." The properly-managed corporate school of the Third World will never, Seltzer and Karger regretted, "produce a Che, a Malcolm, or a Mao to threaten the social order benefitting the corporations."[112]

In April 1974, *Ramparts* published an essay titled "Could Karl Marx Teach Economics in America?" contributed by Lawrence S. Lifschultz, who was a national coordinator of Concerned Asian Scholars, and also a South Asia

---

[111] Michael Seltzer and Howard Karger, "Good Morning Class, My Name is Bzzz Vzz Crackle," *Ramparts Magazine*, March 1974, p. 11.

[112] Ibid, p. 15.

correspondent for *Pacific News Service*. At a moment in history when Marxist economic theory seemed more resonant and relevant than ever to many academics watching the global economy collapse in the wake of the OPEC embargo, some universities seemed to be attempting to purge Marxism from the curriculum. Lifschultz noted that in 1974 the Vietnam war inflation, the downfall of the Bretton Woods international monetary system, a persisting balance of payments problem, and a continuing official unemployment rate of close to five percent, had all but eroded public faith in economists who championed Keynesianist deficit spending.

The public economic crisis exacerbated by the OPEC oil embargo was, Lifschultz wrote, "beginning to come home and the economics profession was itself being shaken by an internal war of ideas pitting orthodox economists against a younger generation of radicals that threatened not just an old and comfortable unanimity, but the very underpinnings of American capitalist theory." Harvard's Economics Department was, for example, witnessing its "worst division in history," created by a decision not to rehire two radical economists. Meanwhile, at Yale, the Economics Department held its third full departmental meeting of the year to deal with the "gnawing problem of Karl Marx."

Students and several younger faculty, Lifschultz explained, insisted that Marxian economics be made a formal part of the Department's curriculum. Further inland at the Amherst campus of the University of Massachusetts, following nearly three years of infighting which included the resignation of two department chairmen, the University made a remarkable job offer and hired five radical economists, four with tenure. John Kenneth Galbraith, President of the American Economic Association, urged his colleagues to "reassociate with reality," and attacked the current orthodoxy in economic theory because it offered "no useful handle for grasping the economic problems that now beset modern society."[113] He wrongly prophesied that "rationality dictated" that those who sought to purge Marxism from a formal education in the field of economics would eventually be purged themselves due to not having a grasp on the "reality of modern economics."

In August 1974, *Ramparts* published an essay titled "Education: Trying Other Ways," contributed by Herbert Kohl, who from 1969 to 1972 taught at Other Ways, an alternative school located in a storefront and affiliated with the Berkeley Unified School District. His essay was an account of his experience and derived from excerpts from his book, *Half the House* (1974). Kohl founded the Open School movement in the 1960s and was credited with coining the term "open classroom." He advocated child-centered education in which a student neither receded

---

[113] Lawrence F. Lifschultz, "Karl Marx Teach Economics in America?" *Ramparts Magazine*, April 1974, p. 27.

from nor indulged blindly in the affairs of the outside world. He believed that the American school system taught children to define success in terms of materialism and negligibly made self-centered citizens in an increasingly global world. Kohl conversely believed that students should, above all, learn to make the world a better place for everyone, which he believed was the true measure of success.

To succeed in changing American culture to become more egalitarian and less materialistic, Kohl believed, "we must pull together, support one another's struggles, and keep a vision of the whole before us." He also lamented the ennui in the New Left, noting that he was often asked whether it was worth beginning again after the sad fate of the civil rights movement, the disenchantment with alternative schools, the resignation and conformity of many university students, the general amnesia about the U.S.'s role in Vietnam, and the cynicism and harshness of the federal government and large corporations manifest in dealing with the needs of poor and powerless people, which was a crises that seemed manufactured to confound and exploit the middle class. The answer, to Kohl, was, "What choice do we have? Either we struggle to create a sane world or destroy ourselves and the earth through greed and thoughtlessness."[114]

Contributors to *Ramparts* often depicted American society during the 1960s and 1970s to be marred by pervasive corruption and an often-overlooked fascism and banality of evil at all strata's of the social system, including in the realm of education, which the editors and contributors to the magazine often, as indicated in the pages above, perceived to be perverted especially by capitalism, materialism, and militarism. These depictions of a fascism deeply embedded in American society was often simply insinuated or alluded to. However, as the next chapter illuminates, there were times when the editors and contributors to the magazine were

---

[114] Herbert Kohl, "Education: Trying Other Ways" *Ramparts Magazine*, August 1974, p. 64.

explicit in their assertions that fascism was a
central aspect of American society.

CHAPTER SEVEN

"The Specter of American Fascism"

Ramparts Magazine often critiqued what editors and contributors to the publication perceived to be fascist characteristics, either implicitly or explicitly, in American imperialism and society writ large. In the spring of 1964, prior to the magazine moving its headquarters from Southern California to San Francisco, *Ramparts* published a symposium including two essays about the John Birch Society. The first, "A Note on the Birch Society," written by John Cogley, and the second, "The Catholic Church and the John Birch Society," written by Stillwell John Connor, both indicated that the JBS, which seemed to be increasingly popular in Southern California in particular, was a fascistic organization.

Cogley, who was a former editor of the Catholic journal, *The Commonweal* and who lived in Rome, described the Birchers as "psychologically sick" and lacking rationality, but hoped they could be reasoned with.[115] He also indicated that JBS was more harmful to the nation than communists. Cogley's essay was followed in the spring 1964 edition of *Ramparts* by the article written by Connor, who a businessman and a member of the Council of the John Birch Society; this Council was a group of twenty-six conservative white men who regularly met with Robert Welch, who headed the JBS, to "evaluate and advise on the Communist threat" and the effectiveness of the organization in combating this so called "evil."

The JBS was established in Indianapolis, Indiana on December 9, 1958, by a group of twelve conservative white men led by Welch, a retired candy manufacturer from Belmont, Massachusetts. Welch named the new organization after John Birch, an American Baptist missionary and military intelligence officer who was shot and killed by communist forces in China in August 1945, shortly after the

---

[115] John Cogley, "A Note on the Birch Society," *Ramparts Magazine*, Spring 1964, p. 12.

conclusion of World War II. Connor wrote about Welch as if he was a cult leader and the religion was anti-communism, which both men seemed terrified of.

The JBS was an especially vitriolic anti-communist organization and opposed the 1960s civil rights movement, claiming that it had Communists in important positions. The JBS also opposed the Civil Rights Act of 1964 and the Equal Rights Amendment of 1965, claiming that they were evidence of the Federal Government overstepping individual states' rights to enact civil rights laws, which many Birchers believed, was also evidence that communists had infiltrated the highest echelons of the American political system. JBS also advocated the impeachment of Chief Justice of the United States Supreme Court Earl Warren. JBS was also an ardent opponent of the United Nations. Many of the organizations members also openly endorsed Barry Goldwater, the Republican Party's 1964 nominee for President of the United States.

The focus shifted from fringe fascist groups such as the JBS to institutional fascism embedded in American society in the August 1965 edition of *Ramparts,* namely in an essay titled "The Fictitious Freedom of the Press," contributed by Howard Gossage, who worked as an advertising agent San Francisco. Gossage argued that the notion of freedom of the press was a misnomer because publication decisions were dictated by selling advertising space, which dictated both the quantity and often substance of content that was designed to facilitate economic exchange. In other words, regardless of the ideology espoused in publications such as *The National Review* or *Ramparts*, both were ultimately designed to sell ad space in order to produce more magazines.

In January 1966, *Ramparts* published an essay titled "The Case of the Spies Who Weren't," written by Rex Stout, who was the author of *The Doorbell Rang* (1965). Stout's essay rehashed the execution of Ethel and Julius Rosenberg in 1954, parents of two young boys who were convicted of treason for allegedly passing atomic secrets to the Soviet Union. Many, including Stout, considered the Rosenberg case and McCarthyism writ large to be glaring evidence of American conformity, fascism, and a banality of evil deeply entrenched in Cold War American society.

In April 1966, *Ramparts* published an opinion column titled "Amerika Uber Alles," written by Christian Geissler, who argued that the American power structure in the Vietnam era was not a dissimilar brand of fascism associated with the Nazis a generation earlier. He noted the glaring irony of the Nuremberg Trials in which the ruling class of a victorious nation attempted to pass judgment on actions resulting from precisely the same motives that led the ruling class itself into power – war.

The realist, Geissler wrote, "must thus conclude that the people on top help each other in the struggle against the advancement of the masses, in the struggle for the preservation of the old power structure, above and beyond Auschwitz and Hiroshima." And it did not matter in the least, he asserted, if the rulers did it with evil intentions or because of the economic or ideological pressures of the system they created. Those in power created the system, he wrote, and that made them "responsible for the consequences." In order to condemn and do away with war in 1945, he explained, it would have been necessary to condemn and change completely the power structure, i.e., the property relationships, throughout the western world. "War will not be abolished by those for whom it benefited," Geissler concluded, in one way or another, profitable — either in the area of "economic power, or in the area of spiritual and intellectual power."[116]

The allusions to the Nazis during World War II and the American Empire in Vietnam continued in the October 1966 edition of

---

[116] Christian Geissler, "Amerika, Amerika Uber Alles," *Ramparts Magazine*, April 1966, p. 7.

Ramparts, namely in an editorial titled "Hitler's Bishops." Many Church leaders, the editors informed readers, either openly supported or remained silent as Hitler and Mussolini rose to power. The editors proceeded to beseech the leaders of the American Catholic Church to publicly condemn America's war in Vietnam, lest they be remembered in the pages of history as "Hitler's bishops' of America."[117]

In October 1966, *Ramparts* published an excerpt from Thomas Merton's *Raids on the Unspeakable* (1964) titled "A Devout Meditation in Memory of Adolf Eichmann," in which the author proffered the notion that there was a deeply embedded banality of evil in America's Cold War corporatist and militarized society. Merton's eulogy of Eichmann continued the theme of comparing the American war in Vietnam as being symptomatic of the same disease suffered by the homicidal and genocidal

---

[117] *Ramparts* editorial staff, "Hitler's Bishops," *Ramparts Magazine*, October 1966, p. 3.

Nazis. Merton, the Christian mystic and peace activist, wrote his meditation on Eichmann as a lamentation on what it meant to be sane in a world gone completely mad with nuclear weapons and war. One of the most disturbing facts that came out in the Eichmann trial, Merton wrote, was that a psychiatrist examined him and pronounced him perfectly sane, which, Merton believed, underscored how mad society was. Eichmann, Merton explained, also had a profound respect for law and order. He was obedient, loyal, and a faithful officer of the state. It was thus, Merton concluded, the supposedly sane ones, the well-adapted ones, who could without qualms and without nausea aim the missile, and press the buttons that would initiate "the great festival of destruction that they, the sane ones, had prepared."[118]

In January 1967, *Ramparts* published an editorial that likened William Wirtz, who was

---

[118] Thomas Merton, "A Devout Meditation in Memory of Adolf Eichmann," *Ramparts Magazine*, October 1966, p. 8.

the U.S. Secretary of Labor from 1962 – 1969, to be a "prime candidate to be a presidential candidate in George Orwell's *1984*" in light of Wirtz's suggestion that military service be made compulsory for eighteen-year-old Americans, a notion backed by Secretary of Defense Robert McNamara, who, like John Kennedy and Lyndon Johnson, considered himself a liberal and progressive.

McNamara had also, the editors recounted, proposed that the Armed Services lower mental and physical standards for acceptance into what would be a compulsory profession as part of a "humanitarian" salvage system for lower income and minority Americans. "McNamara," the editors wrote, "termed an 'inequity' the prospect that these underprivileged kids might otherwise be denied the educational, moral and vocational opportunities that the Armed Forces could provide them."[119]

---

[119] *Ramparts* editorial staff, "*Mr. Orwell, Meet Mr. Wirtz,*" *Ramparts Magazine*, January 1967, p. 8.

The editorial thus underscored how the military was becoming the de facto American jobs program. The military, in short, was one of the few avenues to social mobility for low-income Americans, most especially minorities who also found in the military a path to full recognition as American citizens. The military thus increasingly served as a counterrevolutionary force in American society because it increasingly compelled the greatest potential revolutionaries American society had – poor minorities – into the military, which would help to ensure that the inequality around the globe described by Geissler in "Amerika Uber Alles" would not just endure, but be made possibly by poor Americans.

In January 1967, *Ramparts* published an essay contributed by Bill Turner titled "The Minutemen." In it Turner described an organization comparable in their hatred toward and fear of communism as was the John Birch Society described by Cogley. Turner focused especially on the Minutemen's founder, biochemist Robert DePugh. DePugh and the Minutemen were convinced that communists would soon take over the country. They thus built a white supremacist and fascistic army to prepare for a counterrevolution.

In February 1968, just days after the Tet Offensive and the indictment of Dr. Benjamin Spock for conspiring to "aid, abet, and counsel draft registrants to violate the Selective Service Act," *Ramparts* published an essay titled "The Repression at Home" as a preface to Jean-Paul Sartre's "On Genocide." The editors described America's war in Vietnam as an "example," an admonition to those who would challenge the status of American power. This admonition, the editors explained, was directed at home as well as abroad. The charges levied against Spock and his co-conspirators, including Yale's Chaplain, were "more than a crackdown," the editors asserted; it was a "provocation and, in an important sense, a test." This "test" was, they argued, designed to limit free speech. This new act of repression, the editors asserted, represented a fundamental break with previous handling of opposition to the Vietnam War — and it foreboded "a greater desperation."

Up to 1968, the government had sought, as far as possible, to trivialize dissent rather than to repress the antiwar movement because the government had been terribly anxious to avoid the appearance of a national crackdown, of hysteria, of McCarthyism. It has been careful because, aside from its precarious international image, it did not want to consolidate antiwar sentiment around a decisive case, and it did not want to stimulate the often-impotent forces of civil libertarian liberalism into support for militant opposition to the war. The Spock case would, the editors asserted, undoubtedly be one of the most important political trials in American history. "If Spock and those he "aided and abetted" were conspirators," the editors concluded, "then we must become a nation of conspirators. If we do not stand with them, it is impossible to see where the repression at home, and the oppression abroad, will stop."[120]

This editorial was followed some pages later by Carl Oglesby's description of the conception of Sartre's essay "On Genocide." Oglesby, a former president of Students for a Democratic Society and author of *Containment and Change* (1967), was also a member of the International War Crimes Tribunal, which was called by Jean-Paul Sartre and Bertrand Russell to consider the criminality and amorality of U.S. actions in Vietnam. Among the charges taken up by the Tribunal was genocide.

Genocide, Oglesby explained, presented itself as the only possible reaction to the rising of a whole people against its oppressors. The American government was, he explained, guilty of having preferred a policy of war and aggression aimed at total genocide to a policy of peace, the only policy that could, he asserted,

---

[120] *Ramparts* editorial staff, "The Repression at Home, *Ramparts Magazine*, February 1968, p. 2

really replace the former. A policy of peace would, he explained, necessarily have required a "reconsideration of the objectives imposed by the large imperialist companies through the intermediary of their pressure groups." The ties of the "One World," on which the U.S. hoped to impose its hegemony, had, Oglesby explained, grown tighter and tighter in the 1960s. For this reason, he added, the "genocide in Vietnam was conceived as an answer to people's war and perpetrated in Vietnam not against the Vietnamese alone, but against humanity." The Vietnamese, he noted, fought for all men and the American forces against all... And not only because genocide would be a crime universally condemned by international law, but because little by little the whole human race was being subjected to this genocidal blackmail piled on top of atomic blackmail, that was, to absolute, total war... The group which the U.S. wanted to intimidate and terrorize by way of the

Vietnamese nation was, he concluded, the "human group in its entirety."[121]

In May 1972, *Ramparts* published a eulogy to George Lester Jackson titled "Deaths I Have Known," contributed by Jose Yglesias, who was a journalist and author of *The Truth About Them: Pioneers of Modern U.S. Literature* (1971). While serving a sentence for armed robbery in 1961, Jackson became involved in revolutionary activity and co-founded the Maoist-Marxist Black Guerrilla Family. In 1970, he was charged, along with two other Soledad Brothers, with the murder of prison guard named John Vincent Mills in the aftermath of a prison fight.

In 1970, Yglesias published *Soledad Brother: The Prison Letters of George Jackson*, which was a combination of autobiography and manifesto addressed to "a black American audience." The book became a best-seller and earned Jackson fame. In 1971, he took several

---

[121] Carl Oglesby, "On Genocide by Jean-Paul Sartre," *Ramparts Magazine*, February 1968, p. 42.

guards and two inmates hostage in a bid to escape from San Quentin Prison. However, the incident ended with Jackson being shot and killed by a guard, in addition to the deaths of five hostages. Yglesias contextualized Jackson's death into a larger twentieth century history of what he perceived to be the politically motivated murder of Sacco and Vanzetti, and Julius and Ethel Rosenberg. All these deaths, Yglesias concluded, were evidence of an American fascism that systemically destroyed those with the courage to expose the fascism deeply embedded in American society.

In August 1973, *Ramparts* published an essay titled "The Second Frame-up of Julius and Ethel Rosenberg," which was a review of Louis Nizer's recently published *The Implosion Conspiracy* (1973), contributed by Walter Schneir, who was a co-author of *Invitation to an Inquest* (1965). *The Implosion Conspiracy* did not address itself to the guilt or innocence of the Rosenbergs, who were tried, convicted, and executed for treason in 1954 for allegedly passing atomic secrets to the Russians.

Schneir instead raised an essential legal question: Was there sufficient evidence for the jury to find the Rosenberg's guilty? Nizer argued that there was. Schneir, whose *Invitation to Inquest*, was a kind of defense of the Rosenbergs, argued that Nizer underhandedly edited and condensed trial testimony, without indicating deletions, and so made the stories of prosecution witnesses appear far more lucid and coherent than they actually were.

In 1983, the updated and expanded edition to *Invitation to an Inquest* was published. It contained new chapters based on some 200,000 pages of FBI and other government documents relating to the Rosenberg-Sobell case. These documents were obtained under the Freedom of Information Act by means of an eight-year-long legal battle waged — against the determined opposition of the FBI — by attorney Marshall Perlin on behalf of the Rosenbergs' adult sons, both of whom were active in the New Left. As late as 1983, the FBI was determinedly withheld tens of thousands of files, and substantial proportion of which were heavily censored. Clearly, in working with such rich yet problematic source material, questions of accuracy and authenticity were bound to arise, and some honest differences of interpretation between researchers would hardly be surprising. In other words, despite new evidence that seemed to suggest the Rosenbergs were Soviet spies, the question of their guilt or innocence remained, Schneir believed, shrouded in mystery.

In November 1973, *Ramparts* published a profile titled "The Sons of Julius and Ethel Rosenberg," contributed by Jonah Raskin, who was the author of *The Mythology of Imperialism: A Revolutionary Critique of British Literature and Society in the Modern Age* (1971). Julius and Ethel's sons, Michael and Robert Meeropol, were active members of the New Left and dedicated their lives to defending the innocence of their parents. They were orphaned by the executions and were not adopted by any relatives, many of whom felt compelled to change their names so as to not have to the burden of that Scarlet Letter attached to them in an age of Cold War hysteria towards communism.

A high school teacher, poet, songwriter, and social activist, Abel Meeropol and his wife, Anne, finally adopted the Rosenberg boys. After Martin Sobell's 2008 confession, the Rosenberg's boys reluctantly acknowledged that their father had been involved in espionage, but asserted that whatever atomic bomb information Julius Rosenberg had passed to the Russians was, at best, superfluous; the case was, they reminded critics, riddled with prosecutorial and judicial misconduct; their mother in particular was convicted on flimsy evidence in order to place leverage on her husband, who the government was desperate to get a confession from; and neither, the Meeropol brothers insisted, deserved the death penalty. Michael and Robert later co-wrote a book about their and the lives of their parents, *We Are Your Sons: The Legacy of Ethel and Julius Rosenberg* (1975). Robert also wrote a memoir, *An Execution in the Family: One Son's Journey* (2003). The Rosenberg sons viewed the execution of their parents as evidence of a brand of American fascism in which the nation was willing to use the legal system to destroy political opposition.

In June 1974, *Ramparts* published an essay titled "General Motors and the Nazis," written by Bradford Snell, who was assistant counsel to the Senate Monopoly and Anti-Trust Subcommittee. His essay, which was financed by the Stern Fund, was an excerpt from his report to the Senate Subcommittee on Antitrust and Monopoly. He noted that during the OPEC embargo, the major international oil companies had a curious and dubious dual role to play: 1. as domestic sellers of petroleum products, they were charged with maximizing supplies of crude oil to the U.S.; 2. as agents of the oil producing countries, they were charged with enforcing the cut-off of those same supplies. The seeming

paradox created new political urgency in regard
to the question of whether multinational
corporations should be entrusted with such vital
matters as assuring the availability of energy.

Snell noted that the problems posed by
multi-nationalism were not entirely new. The
astoundingly cynical functioning of America's
automobile giants during World War II was, he
argued, particularly illuminating. He employed
recently declassified military and diplomatic
source materials to document the insidious
extent of wartime "double dealing," especially
on the part of General Motors. Due to their
multinational dominance of motor vehicle
production, GM and Ford both became principal
suppliers for the forces of fascism as well as for
the forces of democracy during the 1930s.

"Had the Nazis won," Snell wrote,
"General Motors and Ford would have appeared
impeccably Nazi; as Hitler lost, these companies
were able to reemerge impeccably American." In
either case, Snell added, "the viability of these

corporations and the interests of their respective stockholders would have been preserved."[122] He concluded by elaborating yet another paradox of the opportunistic, amoral, and fascistic nature of multinational corporations who cared only about the enrichment of shareholders.[123]

Ramparts, as the previous pages indicate, depicted fascism to be entrenched in Cold War American society. But there was also a great deal of room for dissidents to demand basic human rights and that also permitted publications such as Ramparts to exist. In other words, liberty, justice, and equality were in constant tension with corporatist, technocratic, and militaristic impulses. This tension, Ramparts helped to illuminate, shaped American identity and fueled the social conflicts of the 1960s and 1970s. But the American court system, as the next chapter helps to illuminate, was increasingly used as a

---

[122] Bradford Snell, "General Motors and the Nazis," Ramparts Magazine, June 1974, p. 16.

[123] Ibid, p. 16.

counterrevolutionary force in during the
Vietnam War era in American history.

CHAPTER EIGHT

"The Weaponization of American Courts and Prisons"

Ramparts Magazine tended to portray law enforcement agencies and American court system as a diabolical forced designed to undermine political opposition and strangle in the cradle revolutionary elements within the United States. *Ramparts* covered numerous show trials that transpired in the U.S. during the Nixon administration. The first was in April of 1969. It was titled "The Oakland Seven," and written by Terence Cannon and Reese Erlich. The defendants in the Oakland Seven trial were the authors of the article plus Steve Hamilton, Bob Mandel, Mike Smith, Frank Bardacke, and Jeff Segal – the leaders of the 1967 Stop The Draft Week. The Seven faced a total of sixty-one years in state prison on charges of "conspiring to commit two misdemeanors" and assaulting an officer.

The article provided a window into the moment in the antiwar and civil rights movements when dissidents began to abandon non-violent tactics for more direct and confrontational measures. Cannon and Erlich, for example, explained that the protesters they were affiliated with wanted to launch a large-scale protest at the Oakland Draft Induction Center, but were fed up with telling demonstrators to go peacefully into the police vans and to sit still and quiet while getting their heads beat in. Rather than pleading with those in power to please stop killing young men in Vietnam, the young men, Cannon and Erlich wrote, had a "right to try to stop the killings." Released from what they referred to as "the bondage of nonviolence," a lot of people at meetings championed what the essayists described as "fantasies about seizing and holding power, killing cops, cementing closed the doors of the Induction Center, pouring gasoline in the gutters, and stripping nude in front of the police."[124] Their most notable quotes were written down by police spies and would later be attributed to the Oakland Seven when the undercover agents testified before the Alameda County Grand Jury. It was, however, the undercover agents, Cannon and Erlich explained, "who were the most 'militant' of our group."

A week of demonstrations at the Oakland Induction Center was called for October 16 through 20th. The group ultimately decided to interpose their bodies between the Induction Center and the buses bringing the inductees to it. The group had sent telegrams to Governor Ronald Reagan asking them to shut down the Induction Center. "'If you won't,'" the protestors promised, "we will." Reagan raged against what he referred to as "attacks on the fabric of our social structure." Cannon, as such, was arrested for having picket sticks in the trunk of his car

---

[124] Terence Cannon and Reese Erlich, "The Oakland Seven," *Ramparts Magazine*, April 1969, p. 34.

and charged with twenty-nine counts of possession of a lethal weapon – one felony count for each stick.[125] The rest of the protesters were charged with conspiracy, which was defined as, in effect, intent to advocate participation in an assembly of three or more persons where violence could potentially occur.

Use of the conspiracy indictment was part of a general trend in 1960s America to undermine political opposition to the Vietnam War. The government increasingly cloaked in law and order discourse as a means of controlling and eliminating grassroots dissent. The conspiracy law first appeared in the historic Philadelphia Cordwainer's Case of 1806, when the judge ruled that the strike of shoemakers with the object of gaining a salary increase was a "criminal conspiracy." But the tactic became more prominent during the Nixon administration.

In 1968, for example, the federal government chose Dr. Benjamin Spock to serve

---

[125] Ibid, p. 35.

as an example to draft resisters by charging and convicting him of conspiracy to "counsel, aid and abet" draft refusal. The conspiracy law was perfectly suited to political repression because the specific offense need only be discussed and need not actually be committed, which permitted the government to argue that it preemptively defended national security. It was as if the Thought Police prophesied in George Orwell's *1984* had become not just an actual thing, but also a commonly used weapon in 1960s and 1970s.

The Oakland Seven defendants, Cannon and Erlich explained, did not even have to know each other to be charged with conspiring. One or several "conspirators," for example, could be government agents, police officers, or informants, whose job it was to plan a conspiracy. State governments increasingly used local laws, which made the act of demonstrating a misdemeanor, but the planning of demonstrations was a felony. The law was all encompassing and ridden with ambiguity. A discussion by long distance telephone about a demonstration that did not even occur could be made into a felony. The penalty was ten years in prison. Cannon and Erlich concluded the essay by soliciting funds for the Oakland Seven's Defense. The Seven were eventually found not guilty of conspiracy, but the ordeal cost them years of their lives and tens of thousands of dollars defending themselves in the court system, which diminished their ability to be political activists determined to end the war.

In January 1970, *Ramparts* published an introductory editorial titled "Repression and the Chicago Eight" that preceded an article titled "The Chicago Conspiracy Trial" written by Paul Glusman, who was an activist at the University of California at Berkeley. The editors detailed the government's attempt to hold Abbie Hoffman, Jerry Rubin, David Dellinger, Tom Hayden, Rennie Davis, Lee Weiner, and Bobby Seale responsible for the nationally televised "police riot" at the Hilton Hotel, where the Democratic National Convention was held in August of 1968.

Seale had, Glusman explained, been kidnapped, framed, and denied the counsel of his choice and had been physically abused for trying to make his own defense, and then finally sentenced to four years for refusing to "submit in silence to the attempt to railroad him to prison." The four-year sentence for contempt was later overturned.

The editors at *Ramparts* wrote that the lessons of the 1968 Democratic Convention were that the political system was "rigged beyond reform;" that the "armed guardians of the law were there to break the heads of the unarmed conscience of the nation;" and that "brute force reigned at home as well as abroad." The trial of the Chicago Eight, they asserted, shattered the remaining illusions of a rule of law and an independent judiciary, and marked a major advance in a new wave of repression which in numbers jailed (draft resisters and protesters) and killed (blacks, especially Black Panthers) already dwarfed anything seen in the McCarthy era.[126]

The editors quoted W.H. Ferry, a former scholar in residence at the Center for the Study of Democratic Institutions who described the Chicago conspiracy trial as glaring evidence of the United States being a police state. "As layers of broad support are stripped away," the editors wrote, "the radicals who have led the opposition are to be picked off one by one (as in Chicago today) and the country is to be pacified. People must see," they asserted, "the drama of repression being enacted in Chicago for what it was: a threat, not just symbolic, but direct and real, to their own political and social aspirations." Solidarity with the Chicago Eight, with the Panther leaders, and with other radicals singled out for attack, was, they concluded, "an essential priority."[127]

---

[126] *Ramparts* editorial staff, *"Repression and the Chicago Eight," Ramparts Magazine*, January 1970, p. 7.

[127] Ibid, p. 10.

Glusman's article began with a drawing of Bobby Seale bound and gagged in Judge Julius Hoffman's courtroom. The trial continued in Seale's absentia, after he had been charged with contempt of court. Seale, Glusman wrote, did more than anyone to cut through the hypocrisy of the trial and to destroy the facade of judicial impartiality that ordinarily served to cover the political repression that goes on in the courts. Glusman further noted that the trial seemed to be polarizing the country and that it and repression constituted the "preferred strategy of the Nixon administration."

Having put Bobby Seale away, Glusman explained, "the government would like to turn their attention to the antiwar movement, jailing its leaders too." He concluded by explaining that by appointing conservatives to judicial posts (including the Supreme Court), by bringing government pressure into the courtroom, and more generally by rallying the right (the so called silent majority) and publicly attacking dissent, the Nixon administration was already actively working to "create a situation in which political activists could be jailed without the threat of reversals."[128]

The entire July 1970 edition of *Ramparts* was devoted to Tom Hayden's not-yet-published book, *Trial* (1970), which delved deep into the Chicago Conspiracy Trial and its moral and political implications for American society. The first article in the July 1970 edition of *Ramparts* was an editorial titled "A Tract for Our Time." In it the editors ominously described America as being mired in a state of crisis. U.S. troops had, they noted, invaded Cambodia, exposing Washington's determination to stay in Vietnam and increasing the likelihood of war with China and the use of nuclear weapons. National Guardsmen, the editors noted, also still occupied rebellious communities throughout the country; the four white students they murdered at Kent State University had, they declared, become

---

[128] Paul Glusman, "The Chicago Conspiracy Trial," *Ramparts Magazine*, January 1970, p. 47.

martyrs, but the black students killed eleven days after Kent State in Jackson, Mississippi were mostly forgotten — indeed, the editors seethed, they were hardly even noticed by a society "so racist it did not even understand that race war, initiated by the guardians of its law, had already begun." And yet out of this fragmented kaleidoscope of rebellion and repression, they asserted, for the first time young people had glimpsed the potential strength of their "united outrage." The students, the editors asserted, realizing the magnitude of their power, had taken their own course of action by shutting down their universities, colleges and even high schools behind their own radical demands.

These demands included that the U.S. government end its systematic repression of political dissidents and released all political prisoners, such as Bobby Seale and others in the Black Panther Party; that the U.S. government ceased its expansion of the Vietnam War into Laos and Cambodia and that it unilaterally and immediately withdrew all forces from Southeast

Asia; that universities ended their complicity with the U.S. War Machine by an immediate end to defense and counterinsurgency research, ROTC, and all other such programs. In making these demands on a racist, war-bent society, the editors wrote, the students had proved themselves to be far ahead of the liberal politicians who were seeking to channel youthful rebellion into the "cul-de-sac of Establishment politics." The editorial circled back to the crisis created by the DNC in 1968 and subsequent Conspiracy Trial and murder of American college students as glaring evidence that the time for "taking revolution from the realm of utopian rhetoric and into political reality had finally arrived."[129]

The publication of Hayden's book, *The Trial*, in the July 1970 edition of *Ramparts* was, the editors hoped, a salvo in the revolution they hoped to narrate for the New Left. Hayden was

---

[129] *Ramparts* Editorial Staff, "A Tract for Our Time," *Ramparts Magazine*, July 1970, p. 6.

considered to be one of the great American revolutionaries of his era. A founder of Students for a Democratic Society, an early civil rights activist in Mississippi, a community organizer in Newark's black ghetto during the bloody insurrection in the summer of 1966, a victim of the police riot in Chicago in 1968, and one of the Chicago Eight in 1970, Hayden had been an important member of a generation which had moved from the McCarhtyist purges of the 1950s to the militant protests of the 1960s.

In *Trial*, Hayden provided insight into the process that culminated in confrontation with Mayor Richard Daley's brutal police force. Hayden's book was the first complete account by a defendant of what actually transpired inside Julius Hoffman's courtroom: how the "conspirators" differed but were able to come together to plot a common defense; how they "educated" their attorneys; how they reacted to the horrific spectacle of Bobby Seale being bound and gagged. But the book was more than an anecdotal account of one of America's most historic courtroom dramas. Hayden hoped that the trial was to be a turning point for an entire generation, and that his book would be an indictment of a "justice" system which revealed itself to be not only corrupt but also fascistic. *Trial* was thus designed to be both an account of the Chicago Eight conspiracy trial and a primer for revolution addressed to those who saw themselves as revolutionaries – those who had worked unsuccessfully for reform through political channels such as the justice system, but who were actively "moving from the sidelines of history to active, outraged opposition."[130]

The second article in the series published by *Ramparts* in July 1970 chronicling the Chicago Eight Trial was the introduction to Hayden's *Trial*, which explored the days leading up to the police riot at the 1968 DNC. The third essay was titled "1968: Repression." In it Hayden described a generation of white students being radicalized as a result of the student strike at Columbia and

---

[130] Ibid, p. 6.

in the streets of Chicago, and at People's Park in Berkeley, California, "where murderous bullets were unleashed against tender white skin." Hayden asserted that future histories would surely locate the late-1960s as the time when "America's famous democratic pragmatism began hardening into an inflexible fascist core."[131]

The fourth essay in the series was titled "Convention Week 1968." It delved into the tense protests, including the fraught protest at Grant Park on August 28, which lurched towards what Hayden believed was erroneously referred to as a "spontaneous police riot" at the 1968 DNC. The fifth essay was titled "A Generation on Trial," which featured a picture of a Chicago Policeman on horseback chasing down a longhaired hippy running through Grant Park. Hayden argued that the only crime the so-called conspirators had committed was being young and having the

---

[131] Tom Hayden, "From Protest to Resistance I. 1968: Repression," *Ramparts Magazine*, July 1970, p. 12.

"audacity to challenge the staid dogma of the elderly white men who propped up Jim Crow in the South, waged a seemingly winless and endless war in Asia, and served as a counterrevolutionary force throughout the developing world."

The sixth article penned by Hayden in the July 1970 edition of *Ramparts* was titled "Their Identity on Trial." In it he argued that an unintended consequence of the Chicago Conspiracy Trial was that it exposed the fascist nature of the American "justice" system and its perverse political oppression of American citizens. The seventh article contributed by Hayden to the July 1970 edition of *Ramparts* was titled "The Rigging of the Justice System." In it he described the Chicago Eight's pretrial motions in which they asked that the indictment be dismissed because of the unconstitutionality of the law; because of its generality; because of bias in the grand jury; because of irregularities in the selection of the grand jury; and on the grounds of double jeopardy. All the motions were denied.

Despite the absence of his lawyer, who had recently had a serious operation, Bobby Seale was told that he could not represent himself, which was an egregious violation of his civil rights. That, Hayden wrote, plus the "evident insanity of Judge Hoffman" made it clear to the accused that the trial was more of a railroading than they had previously believed possible in the U.S.[132] The railroading was also, Hayden stated, always done in the name of the law.

His ninth article was titled "On Contempt of Court." In it Hayden adamantly objected to the mass media's portrayal of the Chicago Eight's in-court conflict with Judge Hoffman as "anarchic" and evidence of the co-defendants attempts to derail the court system. "Time and again," Hayden wrote, "we were provoked into choosing between speaking out or becoming

---

[132] Tom Hayden, "A Generation on Trial: The Rigging of Justice," *Ramparts Magazine*, July 1970, p. 28.

meek, silent accomplices to our own prosecution."[133]

Hayden's tenth essay was titled "The Jury," which he described as having all of the power in the trial. He expressed regret that he and his co-defendants erred terribly in not thinking more about the effect their daily protests of the proceeding would have on the jurors, who were not political activists.[134] Hayden admitted that the co-defendants hurt themselves by not standing when the judge entered the courtroom; Yippies Abbie Hoffman and Jerry Rubin even wore judges' robes to court one day as an affront to Judge Hoffman and to underscore that the entire trial was theater. Judge Hoffman, however, Hayden explained, symbolized the U.S. court system, as such, the jurors interpreted the disrespect towards Judge

---

[133] Tom Hayden, A Generation on Trial: On Contempt of Court," *Ramparts Magazine*, July 1970, p. 29.

[134] Tom Hayden, "A Generation on Trial: The Jury," *Ramparts Magazine*, July 1970, p. 38.

Hoffman as disrespect for the law, the country, and the jurors themselves.

Hayden's eleventh essay was titled "The Trial in Perspective: Thoughts on Political Trials." In it he put the Chicago conspiracy trial into a global context with the American military industrial complex at the center of the story. He wrote that by acting as if basic rights belonged to all Americans, the defendants exposed the fact that those rights actually only belonged to a few. The defendants' assertion of an equal humanity created their strategy in which they found that America could not be both an empire and a democracy. The American Empire, Hayden explained, required "vast outlays of money and military personnel to protect investments and power interests." As the "backbone of the free world, America was led into support for a network of unpopular reactionary regimes." Given the growth of social revolution as an ineradicable fact of modern times, Hayden wrote, it had thus become imperative that "America become more of a military state, taxing and drafting its own people, and consequently stifling any real aspirations at home." Democratic institutions became as result, he lamented, hollower in the process and "power to the people" became an inevitable revolutionary slogan.[135] Hayden also compared the courts to the Church. Much like the church, the courts were not so much an extension of an almighty and omnipotent God, but rather political entities. "Behind those robes," he wrote, "are men of political motivation: landlords, underworld figures, partisan manipulators." Nearly all of them, he regretted, were white, middle-class, and middle-aged, conservative males. The laws they administered thus favored rich against poor, white against black, "respectable" against non-conformist.[136] He concluded that America had entered an epoch in which dissidents were being

---

[135] Tom Hayden, "The Trial in Perspective: Thoughts on Political Trials," *Ramparts Magazine*, July 1970, p. 39.

[136] Ibid, p. 39.

treated more like "prisoners of war than like political heretics."[137]

Hayden's twelfth essay was titled "Justice in the Streets." In it he urged young people to view the Chicago Conspiracy Trial as what he described as "an opportunity for a collective offensive by our generation against Nixon, Agnew and the Justice Department." The defendants were, he explained, symbols of what millions were going through themselves.[138] He noted that outrage over the trial was translated into violence no less than three times nationally in the previous year lone: in the October "Days of Rage" in the streets of Chicago; at the Washington Moratorium in November; and on The Day After. On these three occasions people fought back "against blows coming down in the courtroom," he wrote, further noting that only "organized" violence came from the Weathermen in September and October of 1969.

---

[137] Ibid, p. 40.

[138] Tom Hayden, "The Trial in Perspective: Justice in the Streets," *Ramparts Magazine*, July 1970, p. 41.

"We never did what the government accused us of in 1968," he wrote, "but the Weathermen did it in 1969... Many Weatherman leaders were shaped by the events of Chicago '68" he explained. When the defendants' legal protests were "clubbed down, they became outlaws." When the defendants' pitiful attempts at peaceful confrontation were overwhelmed, many activists, most notably the Weathermen, adopted the tactic of offensive guerrilla violence. When the defendants' protest against the war failed, "they decided to bring the war home."[139]

Hayden's thirteenth essay was titled "The Limits of Conspiracy." In it he wrote that although the Chicago Seven (and Bobby Seale who had since been granted his own trial) served an important revolutionary function for six months, they had also discovered a lot that was wrong about themselves. "Even though our identity was on trial," Hayden wrote, "even though our habits were truly radical compared to

---

[139] Ibid, p. 42.

those of bourgeois society, that hardly meant that our identity and habits were revolutionary by our own standards." He added, "We were particularly oppressive to women; most of us, though proclaiming to be part of the liberated culture, were involved in all-too traditional relationships with our wives."

He concluded by lamenting that the trial crowded out time for democratic decision-making or the non-exploitative relationships they were "supposed to be building."[140] Hayden explained his rationale by noting that while the seven white conspiracy defendants were at least able to speak, write and freely prepare their defense, Seale was seized on the Berkeley streets, indicted on a trumped up murder charge in Connecticut, secretly driven in chains to Chicago, denied his right to representation, chained, gagged and severed from the case, shipped back to California and then off to Connecticut, where,

---

[140] Tom Hayden, "The Trial in Perspective: The Limits of the Conspiracy," *Ramparts Magazine*, July 1970, pp. 44.

in July of 1970, he faced the electric chair. "If ours was the 'political trial of the century,'" Hayden wrote, "Bobby's Long Trial" had become "the definitive trial of black people in America." Seale, who faced the death penalty, Hayden explained, was "symbolic of black people facing genocide."[141]

Hayden's fourteenth contribution to the July 1970 edition of *Ramparts* was titled "The Eighth Conspirator is a Prisoner of War." In it he argued that Black Panther Bobby Seale, the "eight conspirator," was not a political prisoner; he was a prisoner of war. Nearly thirty Panthers, Hayden explained, had been killed since the Party was founded in 1966. In 1969, the first year of the Nixon administration, more than four-hundred Panthers had been arrested on various charges; police had also attacked Panther offices in Los Angeles, Oakland, Chicago, Des Moines and fifteen other cities. Fred Hampton had been

---

[141] Tom Hayden, "From Resistance to Liberation: The Eighth Conspirator Is a Prisoner of War," *Ramparts Magazine*, July 1970, p. 45.

murdered by Chicago Police as he slept in his bed in the wee hours of the morning with his pregnant girlfriend at his side. Nearly all members of the Panther Party's original Central Committee had, Hayden noted, also been suppressed including killed, jailed or forced into exile. The Justice Department also had, Hayden added, a special task force on the Panthers; Hoover's FBI considered them the greatest single threat to national security; and at least two congressional committees and several grand juries were investigating them in 1970. "The Panthers," Hayden concluded, "are the target not of repression but of an undeclared war." He explained that the Panthers held in jails across America in 1970 were "no different from prisoners held in Santo Domingo, Saigon or any other center of the American Empire."[142]

The final article written by Hayden published by *Ramparts* in the July 1970 issue was titled "From Resistance to Liberation." In it

---

[142] Ibid, p. 46.

Hayden wrote that there was a gap between the children of affluence and the children of squalor. "Our need for a new lifestyle," he wrote, "for women's liberation, for the transformation of work, for a new environment and educational system," could not be described in the rhetoric of Third World revolution where poverty, exploitation and fascist violence were the immediate crisis. "We cannot be black," he wrote, "nor can our needs be entrusted to a Third World vanguard of any kind."

The change toward which the American Left seemed to be inevitably moving was one in which the white world yielded power and resources to an insistent mankind. There was, Hayden declared, no escape — either into rural communes or existential mysticism — from this dynamic of world confrontation.[143] Hayden lamented that many white and middleclass members of the New Left had historically argued

---

[143] Tom Hayden, "From Resistance to Liberation: The New American Revolution," *Ramparts Magazine*, July 1970, p. 55.

that colonial liberation should wait for socialist revolution or be submerged in a black-white working-class coalition. In the same vein, some Panthers argued that the women's movement should wait until blacks were liberated. And though Hayden acknowledged the danger in the fragmentation of special interest groups on the New Left, he also saw that so many people conscious of needing to fight for their own liberation underscored that the epoch he was writing from was defined by a "universal desire for a new social order."

This epoch was, he wrote, "a time when total revolution was "on the agenda." He defined total revolution as not a limited and particular revolution for national identity here, or for the working class there, or for women here— but for all of mankind to build "a new, freer way of life by sharing the world's vast resources equally and fraternally." The American Empire had grown so global in scope, he wrote, that mankind had "for the first time not only a common spirit but a common enemy," which was American imperialism and fascism.[144] He tied the narrative back to the martyrdom of Che Guevara, and to Bobby Seale starring down the barrel of a death sentence for a murder he did not commit, and the Black Panthers in general, who, Hayden wrote, "were the first to raise the battle cry of liberation inside America, the first black revolutionary party with an internationalist perspective, the first to threaten imperialism totally from within."[145]

The upshot of the Chicago Conspiracy Trial was that after a federal trial resulting in both acquittals and convictions, followed by appeals, and reversals, some of the seven defendants were finally convicted, although all of the convictions were eventually reversed. As for Seale, his case was eventually thrown out. On May 25, 1971, Judge Harold Mulvey stunned courtroom spectators by dismissing the charges against Erika Huggins, founder of the New

---

[144] Ibid, p. 62.

[145] Ibid, p. 62.

Haven chapter of the Black Panthers, and Seale saying, "I find it impossible to believe that an unbiased jury could be selected without superhuman efforts."[146] Though each of the eight accused conspirators were eventually able to dodge long-term prison sentences, the weaponized court system had still significantly diminished their ability to combat America's war in Vietnam and to pressure the government to fulfil its promises to African Americans in regard to fostering genuine racial equality.

In September 1970, *Ramparts* published a review contributed by Malcolm Burnstein of a book titled *Minimizing Racism in Jury Trials* (1970), which was edited by Ann Fagan Ginger. "As a practicing lawyer, Burnstein wrote, he had found that securing a fair trial was particularly difficult for any black defendant – militant or not – in civil as well as criminal cases." The problems of black people in America's "color-blind" judicial system, Burnstein argued, involved

---

[146] Neil MacFarguhar, "Harold M. Mulvey, 86, Judge at Tense Black Panther Trials," March 1, 2000.

much more than merely jury prejudice.

Minimizing Racism in Jury Trials, as such, delved deep into the racism embedded in the American court system. Jury lists, for example, were typically made up from voter registration rolls, on which African Americans were represented in disproportionately low numbers. Economic hardship further excluded a disproportionate number of blacks from jury duty. Those black people who did appear in the final group of prospective jurors, the venire, could usually be kept off the jury by means of peremptory challenges for which no reason needed be given. Until these embedded racial biases were diminished, Ginger nor Burnstein, did not foresee any substantive racial equality in American jury trials, especially in an era of "sensationalized black militancy."[147]

---

[147] Malcolm Burnstein, "review of *Minimizing Racism in Jury Trials,* by Ann Fagan Ginger," *Ramparts Magazine*, September 1970, pp. 55.

In June 1973, *Ramparts* published an article titled "Ruchell Magee: The Defense Never Rests," written by Alexandra Close, a San Francisco Bay Area writer, who had covered the Ruchell Magee case for two-and-a-half years. On January 13, 1970, corrections officers shot three black prisoners dead at Soledad Prison in California. On January 17, 1970, four days after the shootings, a 26-year-old prison guard named John Vincent Mills was beaten, dragged up three flights of stairs and tossed to his death. A note found beside his body read "One down, two to go."

Three black inmates were charged with this murder and were transferred to San Quentin Prison to await trial. The three defendants, Fleeta Drumo, John Clutchette, and George Jackson were eventually dubbed the "Soledad Brothers" by the press. Jackson was known at the time to be a political activist and writer. He had also in 1966 found the prison gang known as the Black Guerilla Family, which was an outspoken black power group that targeted the white racist infrastructure of the prison system.

In August 1970, 17-year-old Jonathon Jackson, attempted to negotiate the freedom of the Soledad Brothers (which included his older brother, George) by kidnapping Superior Court judge Harold Haley from the Marin County Courthouse in San Rafael, California. The resulting shootout left four men dead, including both Jackson and Judge Haley. Two others were wounded. The event received intense media coverage, as did the subsequent manhunt and trial of Angela Davis, an ousted assistant professor who had taught at the University of California at Los Angeles. She had loose connections to George and Jonathan Jackson, and the Black Panthers. Davis, in fact, owned the weapons used in the incident.

Magee was scheduled to testify on behalf of James McClain, who was defending himself against the charge of assaulting a guard in the wake of the murder of the San Quentin guards' murder of Fred Billingsly, who had been beaten and tear-gassed to death in his cell earlier in the year. On August 7, 1970, Magee, who was to be a witness at James McClain's trial, went to free three other testifying prisoners from their holding cells. Magee fled with Jackson and the hostages, and was wounded when guards opened fire on the escape van. Magee was charged with kidnapping, conspiracy, and murder. Close's article chronicled Magee's desire for self-representation in court and to prove that he was a "slave" because he was being denied constitutional rights. Magee ultimately pleaded guilty to a charge of aggravated kidnapping for his part in the assault. In return for his plea, the Attorney General asked the Court to dismiss the charge of murder (of Judge Haley). Magee later attempted unsuccessfully to withdraw his plea, and was sentenced in 1975 to life in prison.

In August 1973, *Ramparts* published a series of stories about the weaponization of the American legal system. The first was an editorial written by Paul Jacobs, a writer and an associate at the Institute for Policy Studies, titled "Informers: The Enemy Within, An Analytical Survey." The second was a special report titled "The Gainesville Eight: Dirty Tricks on Trial, A Report From Florida," written by Rob Elder, who was a staff writer for *The Miami Herald*. "From Roosevelt to Truman to Eisenhower to Kennedy to Johnson to Nixon—every President and every President's staff had, Elder wrote, carried out illegal and unconstitutional acts." Their "illegal and unconstitutional acts" were justified as being essential to National Security.[148] Elder argued that the preservation of National Security was also the justification for what he believed to be a railroading of the Gainesville Eight.

The Justice Department prosecuted seven Vietnam Veterans Against the War and one VVAW sympathizer. Organized in 1967, Vietnam Veterans Against the War had moved to the forefront of the antiwar movement by the

---

[148] Paul Jacobs, "Informers: The Enemy Within: *An analytical survey*," *Ramparts Magazine*, August 1973, pp. 21-24

summer of 1972. That's part of the reason VVAW leaders such as Gainesville resident Scott Camil were accused of plotting to "organize numerous fire teams to attack with automatic weapons and incendiary devices police stations, police cars, and stores in Miami Beach, Florida, on various dates between August 21 and 24, 1972," which coincided with the Republican National Convention. The indictment further charged that "the individual co-conspirators would fire lead weights, fried marbles, ball bearings, cherry bombs and smoke bombs at police in Miami Beach ... by means of wrist rocket slingshots and cross bows . . . (and) would disrupt communications in Miami Beach."

The conspiracy was alleged to have been put together at a regional VVAW meeting in May 1972, at the Gainesville apartment of Scott Camil, a University of Florida student and the VVAW state coordinator who had been on two tours of duty with the Marines in Vietnam. Camil was one of the eight indicted, and the government made no secret about contending that he was the leader of the alleged plot. As was the case with the Oakland Seven in 1968, informants had infiltrated the group and often seemed to be the most militant members of the organizations as they attempted to entrap other members, which came to light during both trials. Finally, fourteen months after they were indicted, the Gainesville Eight were acquitted. The jury's verdict seemed to confirm what *Ramparts* maintained all along: that the only real conspiracy was the attempt by the Nixon administration to frame the Gainesville Eight and other antiwar activist groups on bogus charges in the hopes of discrediting or destroying the movement.

In January 1970, *Ramparts* printed a story titled "Race War at San Quentin," written by Robert Minton and Stephen Rice. Minton had taught at San Quentin during the previous year in a program leading to an Associate of Arts degree for inmates. Stephen Rice was a doctoral candidate in psychology at the University of California at Berkeley. He had participated in a group counseling program with inmates at San Quentin and other California prisons.

Minton and Rice argued that what had originally begun as a protest by Black Muslims against San Quentin's prison conditions "quickly veered out of control and developed into full-scale racial warfare."[149] The race war, Minton and Rice explained, divided the inmates and any "attempt to create a united front against the insidious prison power structure" had been abandoned and replaced by fear and suspicion, and the only box score convicts cared about after the "race war" at San Quentin was by color: three blacks murdered and one badly wounded; one white murdered and eight in the hospital. Places like San Quentin were, Minton and Rice wrote, "society's dirty linen," and were kept as far out of public view as possible." The prison was, they argued, a source of embarrassment to the body politic, an indication of the extent of its failure.

---

[149] Robert Minton and Stephen Rice, "Race War at San Quentin," *Ramparts Magazine*, January 1970, p. 18.

But it was also "a metaphor—not only for the human predicament," the essayists concluded, but also for "the way that power shaped men to fit its own ends."[150]

In August of 1970, *Ramparts* published an article written by Eve Pell titled "The Soledad Brothers: How a Prison Picks Its Victims." When Soledad (more properly known as the California Training Facility at Soledad) opened in 1946, it was, Pell explained, touted as a progressive institution. But by 1970, it was sometimes referred to by inmates as the "gladiator school" or the "front line" because of the intensity of the racial hostility, which existed between guards and inmates, and among the inmates themselves. Black prisoners sometimes complained about food being contaminated, urine in their coffee, and similar harassments.

Urine in coffee was, however, Pell asserted, "only the tip of the iceberg at Soledad."

---

[150] Ibid, p. 24.

Rampant racism was also prominent, which had led to a series of murders of black inmates and "to the outrageous framing and prosecution of three others" who had become known as the Soledad Brothers. George Jackson, Fleeta Drumgo, and John Clutchette were erroneously charged with the murder of a white prison guard, John Vincent Mills, at the prison on January 16, 1970. They were accused with murdering Mills in retaliation for the shooting deaths of three black prisoners during a prison fight in the exercise yard three days prior by another guard, Opie G. Miller. The accused stood trial in the very same courtroom in which Ruchell Magee would later be tried on charges related to the murder of Judge Haley. After Jackson's death, on March 27, 1972, a San Francisco jury found that the state of California had failed to completely prove its case and thus acquitted the two surviving Soledad Brothers, Clutchette and Drumgo, of the original charges of murdering a prison guard.

In June of 1971, *Ramparts* published an article titled "Women in Prison," written by Kitsi Burkhart, who was a reporter for *The Philadelphia Bulletin* who had also written extensively on the prison system. She argued that Evelyn Newman, Judy Jacobs, Lydia Amado, Betty Barfield, Connie Powers, Merdas Scott, Ethel Gore, Fran Blackwell, and Junett Jaddy-Bey were all political prisoners. But that, unlike the numerous Black Panthers wrongly incarcerated, including Angela Davis, their stories were largely ignored because they were women. She noted that thousands of women incarcerated in American prisons would have no one waiting for them when released. "In fact," she wrote, "most of them will be shunned as ex-cons and will be denied jobs because of their prison records — even though the offense rarely had any relationship to the position applied for."[151] The upshot of the article was that as dire as *Ramparts* made the court system and prison system seem to be for men, especially

---

[151] Kitsi Burkhart, "Women in Prison," *Ramparts Magazine*, June 1971, p. 20.

African-American men, it was an equally destructive force in the lives of countless American women.

The theme of humanizing American prisoners continued in the December of 1971 edition of *Ramparts*, which, not long after the Attica Prison uprisings, published heartfelt letters written by inmates incarcerated at that institution to loved ones, many of which described deplorable and inhumane conditions. The collection of letters was meant to give a name, face, and sense of humanity to those removed from the mainstream of American society.

In February 1972, *Ramparts* published an essay titled "Organizing Behind Bars," written by Frank Browning. The demands made by inmates at Folsom and Attica, he explained, included declaring that being permitted but two-hour visiting periods twice a month constituted inhumane treatment, and that surgeons assisted by unlicensed inmates often equaled murder in the operating rooms of America's prisons, and that isolation of writ writers or those who received political papers amounted to political persecution. Inmates' concerns, in short, focused on power and human oppression. And by referring to themselves as the "the convicted class," Browning wrote, activist prisoners were offering a "clear exposure of how American prisons were used as political tools."

Browning provided a number of statistics that showed how crime adversely impacted the poor and that most inmates were in jail for non-violent offenses. "Though poor people more often go to prison," he wrote, "they are not the biggest thieves." He elaborated that The President's Commission broke down the cost as follows: white collar crimes in 1965 (embezzlement, fraud, tax fraud and forgery) amounted to $1.7 billion while crimes of the poor (robbery, burglary, auto theft, and larceny) came to $608 million. But white-collar criminals, Browning pointed out, almost never went to prison. There were, he explained, plenty of explanations for why white-collar workers almost never went to prison. Most of the reasons boiled down to a fairly simple axiom: they had the money to buy lawyers who could make deals with the District Attorney or the judge, and when they did go to court, they had the requisite class position to win sympathy from juries of their economic peers. Poor prisoners, Browning argued, were also often political prisoners because so many were sent to jail because of the way the political, economic and legal systems "worked" to deny them fair access to the judicial machine. Browning concluded by championing groups like the United Prisoners Union, which was determined to address the inveterate racism and corruption deeply rooted in the American judicial system.[152]

The final article explicitly critiquing the American prison system that *Ramparts* published appeared in the April 1973 edition of the magazine. It was titled "Death on the Yard: The

---

[152] Frank Browning, "Organizing Behind Bars," *Ramparts Magazine*, February 1972, p. 45.

Untold Killings at Soledad & San Quentin," written by Min S. Yee. The article detailed the murder of W.L. Nolen on January 13, 1970. In the summer of 1969, Nolen, a twenty-year-old inmate at Soledad who had been convicted in a 1963 robbery, began circulating a petition to file a lawsuit against the prison's superintendent, Cletus J. Fitzharris, charging that guards and officials at the facility knew of existing social and racial conflicts and that they had been seeking to "excite them through direct harassment and in ways not actionable in court," including the filing of false disciplinary reports and intentionally leaving black inmates' cells unlocked to put them in danger of assault. Nolen also claimed that officials were "willfully creating and maintaining situations" that created and posed "dangers [sic] to the plaintiff [himself]" and that he "feared for his life."

On January 13, 1970, corrections officer Opie G. Miller shot three black prisoners dead at Soledad. Nolen was among the slain, along with Cleveland Edwards, then 21, who had been convicted in 1967 of assaulting a police officer, and Alvin Miller, then 23, who had been convicted of robbery. According to Ellsworth Ferguson, an administrative assistant to Warden Fitzharris at the time, a fight began during a scheduled exercise period for fifteen inmates from the maximum-security wing of the prison. During the conflict, two white inmates among the group were beaten to the ground and Miller was reportedly "fearful that several might be seriously hurt or killed." Officials later stated that it was "surmised" that the fight was racial in nature. Officer Miller, an expert marksman shouted and blew a whistle but gave no warning shot before firing on Nolen, Edwards and Alvin Miller.

White inmate, Billy D. Harris, then 23, who was serving time for assault and perjury, was injured. According to statements made by inmates, there had been an intentional mixing of white prisoners who were known racists and black prisoners in the yard and that some manner of fight had been anticipated. The congregation of the fifteen men in the prison yard had been the first integrated exercise period in several months. The death of a black inmate, Clarence Causey, who had been stabbed to death in 1968, had left racial tensions running high, and for several months prior to January 13, 1970, inmates had only been allowed exercise in the yard one at a time. Furthermore, inmates claimed that the guards had intentionally barred them from taking the wounded prisoners to the hospital, allowing the three shooting victims to bleed for nearly twenty minutes before they were finally taken to receive medical aid.[153]

Ramparts Magazine's coverage of the American courts and prison system during the 1960s depicted "law and order" as a rhetorical device used to justify the continued oppression of poor Americans, particularly African Americans. The legacy of racism and poverty that has always existed in the American system

---

[153] Min S. Yee, "Death on the Yard: The Untold Killings at Soledad & San Quentin, *Excerpts from a Book,"* *Ramparts Magazine*, April 1973, pp. 36.

remained largely ignored and unaddressed by the mainstream American media well into the twenty-first century. But *Ramparts* consistently depicted the justice system and prison industrial complex to be a counterrevolutionary force in American society.

CHAPTER NINE

"Political Corruption in Cold War America"

Ramparts Magazine often depicted the corporate corruption and inequality embedded in American capitalism to be aided and abetted by crooked politicians within a corrupt polity. In January 1967, for example, *Ramparts* published an essay titled "Johnson and the Oil Men," written by Robert G. Sherrill, who was the author of *The Accidental President* (1967). Sherrill's essay consisted of a drawing of one of President Lyndon Johnson's droopy eyes in a triangle atop a pyramid (like the one on the one-dollar bill). The stone bricks in the pyramid had the logo of Gulf, Esso, Phillips 66, and Chevron etched into them.

Sherrill argued that President John F. Kennedy had been, unlike Johnson, committed to reforming the oil industry. The Johnson administration had no such interest, Sherrill argued, in reforming the oil industry. The ease with which mergers were consummated and anti-trust actions dropped under the Johnson administration, were, Sherrill wrote, so pervasive that an observer ran the risk of seeing something "sinister" in the "ease with which the government capitulated to the whims of oil men." It was, Sherrill asserted, even easier when one discovered that in 1964, compared to 1960, Democratic presidential campaign contributions by members of the American Petroleum Institute went up four-hundred percent. The major oil companies had, Sherrill noted, always prospered with Johnson's help. Now that he was President, they could "relax," certain that there would be no presidential tampering with the depletion allowance, no nonsense about opening up the oil import program to competitive bidding, no end runs around the seats of the mighty by annoying state legislators and small, independent oil men.[154]

In September 1967, *Ramparts* published a scathing op-ed written by Sidney E. Zion titled "Here Come De Judge." Zion chronicled an

---

[154] Robert G. Sherrill, "Johnson and the Oil Men," *Ramparts Magazine*, January 1967, p. 40.

several conflicts of interests and glaring evidence of cronyism that could be deduced in Lyndon Johnson's appointment of his former lawyer, Abe Fortas, to the Supreme Court. Fortas, Zion noted, continued to act as an advisor and defender of Johnson even after he had been confirmed by the Senate to sit on the court, thereby "knocking down a wall separating the executive and judicial branches." Fortas was, in Zion's assessment, a microcosm of the endemic political corruption that existed in the American polity during the Vietnam War era. Fortas was ultimately forced to resign from the Court when he was discovered to be a paid consultant to a convicted criminal.

The theme of Johnson's corruption continued in the December 1967 edition of *Ramparts* in an essay titled "LBJ's Favorite Construction Company," written by David Welsh. Johnson's favorite construction company, Welch argued, was the mammoth Brown & Root Inc., owned by George Rufus Brown, who was one of the richest men in the world and a close

friend and longtime business-political associate
of Johnson. The Browns were the principal
financiers of Johnson's early rise to power in
Texas and Johnson was the man who more than
anyone else had, Welch argued, made the
Browns incredibly rich. Brown & Root's
ascension from "penny ante Texas road builder"
to the world's third largest construction
company — which numbered among its contracts
a piece of the $1.6 billion base construction
program in Vietnam — was, Welsh argued, "no
accident and no Horatio Alger story." It was the
story of a politician and a business, on the make
together. When Senator Johnson introduced a
joint resolution on acceleration of military
construction in 1958, Welsh explained, the main
objectives of the resolution were to reduce
unemployment and to put America's productive
facilities to fuller use, which in translation meant
a government subsidy to the giants of the
defense industry. Such was the degree of
concentration that the top nine prime military
contractors in 1966 accounted for twenty-five

percent of the total $33.5 billion allocated for defense contracts. The Brown & Root-Johnson team was, Welch asserted, a case study of corporate control over American political life. Their connivance in the decades between World War II and Johnson's ascendency to the White House may have been more blatant than usual, Welsh concluded, but it was not exceptional: it was representative.

The relentless muckraking of the Johnson administration by *Ramparts* continued in the May 1968 edition in an article titled "LBJ & the Racketeers," written by Michael Dorman, who covered Texas politics for ten years as a reporter for *The Houston Press*, and had more recently worked for *Newsday*. Published shortly after Johnson's shocking decision to not seek reelection, Dorman wrote that to understand the President's rise to power it was imperative to understand the milieu in which he rose – the dirty streets of Houston and Beaumont, Waco and Austin, San Antonio and Dallas, in which his political strength had always been rooted. The oilmen, the politicians, the construction firms and organized crime – had, Dorman explained, all grown up in Texas together in "an orgy of mutual back-scratching."[155] As corrupt as the Tammany Hall Machine of the nineteenth century, Johnson's network reached not only across the cities of Texas but into the highest marble offices of Washington, D.C.

In October of 1968, *Ramparts* published an essay titled "A Welfare State for the Rich [The Platform of the Trojan Donkey]," written by Lee Webb. Webb noted that one of the biggest government subsidies went directly to the oil industry. The 27.5 per cent oil depletion allowance in particular permitted oilmen to avoid many federal taxes. In 1965, for example, one of the twenty largest oil companies — Atlantic — paid no federal income taxes, and four others — Cities Service, Sinclair, Pure and Richfield — paid no taxes and wound up with a tax credit. The average tax rate paid by the

---

[155] Michael Dorman, "LBJ & the Racketeers," *Ramparts Magazine*, May 1968, p. 26.

twenty oil firms that year was 6.6 per cent. If the $5.6 billion profit for that year had been taxed at the normal forty-eight per cent corporate rate, the close to $3 billion dollars saved could have allowed reductions in taxes for the poor.

Big businessmen also, Webb explained, kept a watchful eye on the income tax in Washington. High priority was, he wrote, given to maintaining tax loopholes wide enough to allow high-paid tax attorneys elbow room to neutralize the high-income tax rates for the rich. In 1962, Webb noted, three taxpayers who earned more than five million dollars that year didn't pay any taxes. Nor did three taxpayers with incomes between two and five million dollars, or five with incomes between one and two million dollars, or sixteen who earned between $500,000 and one million dollars. Escaping taxation, it seemed to Webb, proved a man was a professional. And behind each professional, there were tens of thousands of others in the top income brackets who used tax loopholes (and fraud) to escape the income tax that funded

America's war in Vietnam, among other things. Webb concluded by elaborating the great and terrible lengths of hypocritic Democrats in Washington went to speak about closing the tax loopholes exploited by wealthy businessman and corporations while doing all in their power to ensure that nothing changed.[156]

In March 1970, *Ramparts* published an essay titled "Nixon: With A Little Help for His Friends," written by journalist Bob Fitch. The article featured a cartoon of Nixon wearing nothing but short shorts. His body was covered in tattoos such as "Checkers," "SEC," "Silent Majority," "Wall Street," and "Mutual Funds," as he stood awkwardly atop a neoclassical monument with an inscription inscribed in the façade that read: "Political Morality Laugh-In."[157] Fitch noted the 1960 Democratic National Committee advertisement depicting a smarmy

---

[156] Lee Webb, "A Welfare State for the Rich [The Platform of the Trojan Donkey]," *Ramparts Magazine*, October 26, 1968, pp. 35-37.

[157] Bob Fitch, "Nixon: With A Little Help for His Friends," *Ramparts Magazine*, March 1970, pp. 59.

Nixon with a shit-eating grin pasted to his huckster face with bold print text that queried, "Would You Buy a Used Car From This Man?" But by 1968 Nixon was, Fitch argued, not interested in or concerned with appealing to poor or black voters. He had gone all-in on appealing to massive corporations as the bedrock of his campaign's support. "Some people can trust Nixon," Fitch wrote. "But they don't buy their cars in used-car lots."[158] Fitch predicted that the stock market under the Nixon administration would likely implode because the economic climate was eerily similar to the economic climate under the Herbert Hoover administration in the days before the 1929 Stock Market Crash, including high regressive taxes, high interest rates, and high unemployment. The complacent indulgence of President Nixon in the face of impending economic doom could only be "unscrambled," Fitch wrote, as an expression of the "dubious political principles" spelled out in Nixon's recent letter to Wall Street. As candidate,

---

[158] Ibid, p. 65.

Nixon promised Wall Street that if elected he would do all in his power to prevent new "wide sweeping" regulatory powers from being exercised over the mutual fund industry. As President, Nixon delivered on his promise. President Nixon thus took regulation out of the constraints of law and bureaucracy and put it in the context of "hotel room deals and personal favoritism," as did Johnson before him.

In February 1972, *Ramparts* published an article written by James Ridgeway titled "Corporate Tax Bonanza." He argued that Nixon's newly minted tax package provided a subsidy to corporations of $7.5 billion annually, or more than the total budgets of HUD, the Environmental Protection Agency, State Department, and federal judiciary combined. It also exceeded the $5.8 billion proposed in the welfare program and was equal to a $100 cash credit for each individual tax payer in the nation.[159] The article also included a cartoon

---

[159] James Ridgeway, "Corporate Tax Bonanza," *Ramparts Magazine*, February 1972, p. 6.

depiction of Nixon arm-in-arm with utilities and oil companies, which seemed meant to underscore the point that the Nixon administration had aided massive corporations and their lobbyists in seizing the reins of the American polity.

In June 1972, *Ramparts* published an essay titled "Fat Cats and Democrats," written by G. William Domhoff, who had written several books on the American power structure, including *Who Rules America* (1968). With the exception of a Teddy Kennedy or a Jay Rockefeller, Domhoff wrote, no Democratic Presidential candidate could run the fabulously expensive gauntlet that began in the primaries unless he was "adopted by the fat cats of New York, California, and Texas." Domhoff organized his article by focusing on the Jewish Fat Cats from New York, then the Cowboy Fat Cats from Texas, then the gentiles from California. He concluded the article with a section that focused on the lawyers that permitted "fat cats" to commandeer the American polity. What,

Domhoff rhetorically asked readers, did these fat cats get for their money invested into the DNC? First, and most crucially, he explained, they played a major role in determining the party's Presidential candidate.

The fat cats were, Domhoff elaborated, especially essential because no other group within the Democratic Party was able to raise the necessary funds to win a presidency. The Northern liberals usually did not, he noted, have the resources to back a Presidential campaign as well as they did Eugene McCarthy's in 1968, when $11 million in antiwar money was raised. As for the Southern conservatives, they would not, Domhoff asserted, be interested in financing a half-way presentable candidate even if they could. And the trade unions were strictly "bit players" when it came to financing Presidential politics, especially at the level of primary elections. So a Democratic Presidential hopeful, he explained, had to be acceptable to the Jews and the Cowboys to have a chance of winning. And when it came to big offices, "heavy money had very good strings on any successful Democratic candidate," which meant the oil men would continue to enjoy their depletion allowances, the real-estate operators would retain their lucrative depreciation write-offs, and the regressive tax structure would remain an issue that was rarely discussed no matter which party held the balance of power. The political analysts, Domhoff surmised, might have been right that the Democratic Party was "fragmented," and that it presented different varieties of platforms and political activists at the local, state, and national levels. But it was also true, he concluded, that the same few wealthy men decided which of the candidates would receive the millions of dollars that were a "necessary minimum" in major primary and general elections.[160]

In April of 1973, *Ramparts* published an investigative report titled "Disability Pay: The

---

[160] G. William Domhoff, "Fat Cats and Democrats," *Ramparts Magazine*, June 1972, p. 45.

Check at the End of the Tunnel," written by Mark McIntyre, who was a Washington D.C.-based reporter. He found widespread fraud in disability pay amongst Air Force Officers. For example, Alonzo Towner, the 62-year-old the surgeon general of the Air Force, had a strenuous biweekly workout that consisted of a vigorous swim, a set of calisthenics, and then a warm steam-bath. But when he retired from the Air Force in August of 1972, General Towner was declared one-hundred percent disabled. Because of his disability, the general's $26,000 retirement salary was tax-free. The surgeon-general, his subordinates discovered, was afflicted with skin cancer and circulatory problems. Of course, until his retirement, Towner's ailments had not been serious enough to keep him from drawing about $2,000-a-year in hazardous duty pay supposedly available only to those able to pass the Air Force's rigorous flight physical.

Towner's "good fortune" was not, McIntyre asserted, an isolated case. A check of notable Air Force retirees of recent years had turned up case after case where seemingly healthy generals were suddenly found to be seriously disabled. For example, Major General John D. Lavelle, who retired in the summer of 1972 after his private air war against unauthorized North Vietnamese targets became public, paid taxes on less than $3,000 of his $27,000 retirement salary. The reason was, McIntyre explained, because military doctors discovered during Lavelle's retirement physical that the general had a heart murmur, emphysema and a slipped disc. He was thus declared seventy percent disabled. Several months earlier, however, Lavelle had passed his physical and qualified for flight pay.

But, McIntyre wrote, you did not have to be a "bigwig" to benefit from the Air Force's retirement procedures. Recent official figures showed that a majority of the Air Force generals who had retired since 1968 left the service with at least some disability and most of them got thirty percent or more. Meanwhile, fewer than twenty percent of Air Force retirees of all ranks were found disabled. This imbalance was, McIntyre noted, made more striking by the fact that generals frequently performed a dazzling pirouette from hazardous duty flight pay (supposedly requiring tip-top shape) one day to tax free disability (supposedly requiring significant impairment) the next. There was also, McIntyre elaborated, one other catch in disability pay. Many younger two-star generals and admirals who retired with partial or total disability were so handled because there was no more room at the top. Some generals and admirals were thus genuinely surprised to learn that they had been declared disabled (no doubt through hints and direct orders to medical examiners during annual check-ups) but they were forced to take the big pay-off and to retire due to there not being any promotions available.[161]

---

[161] Mark McIntyre, "Disability Pay: The Check at the End of the Tunnel," *Ramparts Magazine*, April 1973, p. 15.

In May 1973, *Ramparts* published an essay titled "Locked Out: Our Last Days at OEO: A Personal Case History," written by Tom Mack and Tim Hoffman, who had been director and deputy director of the Office of Legal Services, San Francisco region (including California, Arizona, Nevada, Hawaii and Micronesia). Hoffman also served as president of Local 3009 of the American Federation of Government Employees, the San Francisco Office of Economic Opportunity union. The OEO was the agency responsible for administering most of the War on Poverty programs created as part of Johnson's Great Society, which, along with the OEO, was gradually dismantled during the 1970s during the Nixon and Ford administrations. "Two non-political lawyers running a successful regional office just wouldn't do," the authors sardonically wrote. "We didn't fit in."[162] Under Nixon, they explained, the top jobs at the OEO had become the dumping ground for political

---

[162] Tom Mack and Tim Hoffman, "Locked Out: Our Last Days at OEO: A Personal Case History," *Ramparts Magazine*, May 1973, p. 19.

hangers-on who lacked the clout for a fat job elsewhere in the bureaucracy. OEO was, they noted, so top-heavy with political pay-off jobs that one out of every thirty-eight employees was a politically sponsored "SuperGrade," making $32,000 or more a year. In other words, the Nixon administration was systemically removing workers at the agency dedicated to administering help to poor Americans in order to install cronies determined to undermine the OEO's mission.

In March 1974, *Ramparts* published an editorial titled "Elk Hills: The New Teapot Dome." In 1912, the Taft administration issued an executive order, which set up Federal reserves of oil for use in case of national emergency, i.e., war. In 1974, there were four Federal Naval Petroleum Reserves: Teapot Dome, Wyoming; Buena Vista, California; the North Slope of Alaska; and Elk Hills, California. Teapot Dome, while instructive as a model of oil industry/government machinations and corruption, was actually, the editors explained, "small game" compared to Elk Hills and the

North Slope. Elk Hills, located about sixty miles northeast of Santa Barbara, comprised seventy-two square miles of rolling hills containing 1,050 wells which, until 1974, produced roughly 2,500 barrels daily for test and maintenance purposes. The potential reserves, according to estimates by the General Accounting Office, were a minimum of 1.3 billion barrels (possibly even as much as 10 billion) of low-sulfur, easily reached petroleum. When the reserve at Elk Hills was first established, the government recognized prior private holdings in the area, including land and mineral rights owned by Standard of California (SoCal) and other oil companies. But in the 1940s, the Navy, in an attempt to regain much of the SoCal-owned land, precipitated a struggle, which resulted in a government-imposed settlement. The upshot was a complicated legal arrangement known as the Unit Plan, which established that the Navy and SoCal Oil would jointly operate the land. If commercial development came, both parties presumably would profit in proportion to their percentage of holdings, which in SoCal's case came to about twenty-two percent.

In November 1973, in his Emergency Energy Address in wake of the OPEC embargo that began a month prior, Nixon called for the official opening up of Elk Hills. Acting on the findings of the Secretary of the Navy, using the justification of national defense needs, Nixon estimated that in the not-too-distant future Elk Hills could produce 160,000 barrels of oil daily, which was approximately eight percent of current shortages. The opening of the field was, the editors asserted, the government subsiding the privatization of massive oil reserves that had presumably belonged to the proverbial people of America. SoCal's sales for 1972 totaled almost $6 billon, with a net profit after taxes of $547 million. At the end of the third quarter of 1973, SoCal already had profits of $561 million, or an eighty percent leap over the equivalent period of the previous year. In other words, the rhetoric of "oil crisis" propagated by the Nixon administration allowed private oil companies to reap windfall profits. They were, like the banks, too big to fail and subsidized by the corporate welfare provided by the American taxpayer.

And the Navy, the editors lamented, saw nothing wrong in allowing the SoCal Oil company to obtain the contract, valued at a minimum of some $10 billion (and rising in value as world oil prices grew ever higher), for actual operation of the most valuable oil resource in the lower forty-eight states. The moral of the story, the editors wrote, might be that the oil industry had become much more sophisticated in getting what it wanted. They further noted that the oil cartel was Nixon's largest contributor to his 1972 reelection campaign. Nixon's friend, David Packard, who was formerly Secretary of Defense and a member in good standing of the board of SoCal, donated $50,000; David Miller, who was also a board member of SoCal, gave the Nixon campaign an equivalent sum. It was thus glaringly evident, the editors concluded, that the oil industry must be "carefully watched," for it had consistently ignored the public interest and bent the laws to suit its grand designs. The corruption at the root of the Teapot Dome Scandal was thus, the editors warned, not just a passage in a history book; that kind of greed and corruption continued to haunt American society in the 1970s.

"Elk Hills: The New Teapot Dome" was immediately followed by an editorial titled "...And in the Mountains of Colorado." It continued the theme of corporations exploiting American taxpayers and concomitantly exploiting the environment in the form of strip mining for oil shale in Colorado, which released numerous toxins into the atmosphere, which destroyed large swaths of the state's ecology, which displaced Colorado's wildlife.

In June 1974, *Ramparts* published an essay titled "Campaign Reform: To Be Taken with a Grain of Salt," written by Robert Walters, who was a national political reporter for *The Washington Star-News*. "Despite all the sanctimonious talk about cleaning up campaign finances," he wrote, Watergate was more likely to produce "mind-bending gimmickry than substantive reforms."[163] Walters believed that the fallout from Watergate would actually make the American polity more corrupt because rather than there being substantive reform, corrupt corporations and the politicians in their pockets would only become more secretive and devious. Corporations, which did not have to worry about being voted out of office, Walters explained, would put all of their resources into defeating campaign finance reform. "We're all probably in for a great deal of ducking, bobbing and weaving on the part of politicians who don't want to be dragged into any scandals in the immediate future, Walters rightly predicted, "and for a return to the great American political tradition of business as usual in the long run."[164]

---

[163] Robert Walters, "Campaign Reform: To Be Taken with a Grain of Salt," *Ramparts Magazine*, June 1974, p. 9.

[164] Ibid, p. 9.

In October of 1974, just before the mid-term elections, *Ramparts* published an essay titled "What We Don't Know Can't Hurt Them," written by Richard Hall. Hall's essay explained the Freedom of Information Act. The original Freedom of Information Act (FOIA) became law in 1966 and, although it had far too many loopholes, was an important first step. People who knew about the law could get a wide variety of information from public agencies; and when those agencies refused to reply, a petitioner with access to legal skills had a chance to win an answer in court. For example, successful court actions forced the FBI to release its directives on the COINTELPRO campaign against the New Left; forced the National Highway Traffic Safety Administration to release correspondence with automobile manufacturers regarding defects; and forced the Department of Housing, Education, and Welfare to release survey reports on the qualifications of local health care facilities.

But, as Hall pointed out, a central flaw in the old FOIA was the wide range of broadly worded exceptions to public access. This was, he noted, particularly the case with classified documents, inter-agency or intra-agency memoranda, and investigative files compiled by almost any government office, agency or bureau. In October 1974, Hall awaited a new FOIA that would, he hoped, close these loopholes. "The government is not about to nail open its doors," he conceded, "but neither can it bolt them shut. Secrets will still exist; the arrogance of officials and bureaucrats will always be with us. But Freedom of Information is the law." And if people learn to assume that they have "the right to ask questions, there will be a lot more answers to go around."[165]

Despite Hall's optimism, President Gerald Ford ultimately vetoed the Privacy Act of 1974 after White House Chief of Staff Donald Rumsfeld, deputy Dick Cheney, and Antonin Scalia of the Office of Legal Counsel persuaded him to do so. However, on November 21, the

---

[165] Ibid, p. 20.

lame-duck Congress overrode President Ford's veto, giving the U.S. the core Freedom of Information Act still in effect today, with judicial review of executive secrecy claims.

The Privacy Act of 1974 amendments to FOIA granted Americans citizens (1) the right to see records about [one]self, subject to the Privacy Act's exemptions, (2) the right to amend that record if it was inaccurate, irrelevant, untimely, or incomplete, and (3) the right to sue the government for violations of the statute including permitting others to see [one's] records unless specifically permitted by the Act. In conjunction with the FOIA, the Privacy Act of 1974 had been used to further the rights of an individual gaining access to information held by the government. Though it became effective in 1967, FOIA seemed to have new importance in the wake of the devious secrecy at the root of the Watergate Scandal. "Information is power when kept firmly in government hands," Hall concluded, and "the erosion of Nixon's presidency, for example, followed step by step his loss of control over the evidence against him."[166]

Also in October of 1974, *Ramparts* published an article titled "The Politics of Common Cause: An Indelicate Balance," written by William Chapman, who was a reporter for *The Washington Post*. Common Cause was a watchdog group founded in 1970 by Republican John W. Gardner, who was the former Secretary of Health, Education, and Welfare in the Johnson administration. Chapman was also a former chair of the National Urban Coalition, an advocacy group for minorities and the working poor in urban areas. As initially founded, Common Cause was prominently known for its efforts to bring about an end to the Vietnam War and lower the voting age from 21 to 18. The organization's tagline was "holding power accountable" and its stated mission was to work to create open, honest, and accountable

---

[166] Richard Hall, "What We Don't Know Can't Hurt Them," *Ramparts Magazine*, October 1974, p. 18.

government that served the public interest; promoted equal rights, opportunity, and representation for all; and empowered all people to make their voices heard in the political process."

As glad as Chapman was that the organization existed, he wondered how much impact it could genuinely have in initiating substantive reform. It was, Chapman concluded, worthy to have the names of lobbyists disclosed, along with the amount of money they spent to buy votes in a state legislature.[167] But he doubted that such knowledge would ever really prevent votes from being bought. He also found it irksome that an organization such as Common Cause had to exist at all. It was, he wrote, "disturbing" to think that on the eve of America's Bicentennial, aroused citizens were forced to demand that committees of Congress be opened to the public or that politicians be

---

[167] William Chapman, "The Politics of Common Cause: An Indelicate Balance," *Ramparts Magazine*, October 1974, p. 44

forced to disclose their sources of financial support. "These seem to be such elementary expectations," he said, "such minimal demands. This may be the real measure of our impatience with Common Cause — that it is around now to settle those accounts we thought were settled long ago."[168]

Though *Ramparts* tended to avoid stories prominently covered by publications such as *The New York Times* and *The Washington Post,* which were considered to be at the mainstream of American society, the editors of *Ramparts* were far too invested in exposing the endemic corruption that existed in the American political system to simply leave the Watergate Scandal to Bob Woodward and Carl Bernstein. As such, the magazine published a handful of articles about Watergate of Watergate operatives, such as G. Gordon Liddy, who has since become something of a cult figure amongst conservative Republicans.

---

[168] Ibid, p. 44.

The Watergate Scandal was perhaps the best-known case of political corruption in American history. It occurred during the early 1970s, following a break-in by five men at the Democratic National Committee headquarters at the Watergate office complex in Washington, D.C. on June 17, 1972, and President Richard Nixon's administration's subsequent attempts to cover up its involvement. After the five burglars were caught and the conspiracy was discovered, Watergate was investigated by the U.S. Congress. Meanwhile, the Nixon administration resisted its probes, which led to a constitutional crisis, and ultimately his resignation from office on August 9, 1974.

In September 1967, more than a year before Nixon was elected President, *Ramparts* foreshadowed the Watergate break-in when the magazine published a sardonic tutorial on how to bug a phone titled "The Case for Bugging," written by Hal Lipset. *Ramparts* had a long history of criticizing the Central Intelligence Agency's and Federal Bureau of Investigation's extralegal measures to undermine perceived enemies of the American power structure, particularly the New Left.

In April 1973, in the midst of Nixon's obstructing of justice in the midst of the Watergate Scandal, *Ramparts* published an editorial article written by Edward Sorel and Kirkpatrick Sale titled "A Modest Proposal: On Increasing Respect for the Presidency." Their essay seemed inspired by the absurdity of partisan conservatives who assailed liberals for "not respecting" the American system and liberals' acrimony towards the President, who had created a Constitutional Crisis in the first place. Respect, Sorel and Kirkpatrick argued, "must be earned, not merely conferred."[169] The conferring of respect and lack of honest and critical thinking by partisan Republicans was,

---

[169] Edward Sorel and Kirkpatrick Sale, "A Modest Proposal: On Increasing Respect for the Presidency," *Ramparts Magazine*, April 1973, p. 34.

they asserted, what emboldened Nixon's corruption.

In August 1973, *Ramparts* published another editorial titled "Watergate." Nixon, the editors asserted, had been caught on the cusp between two periods of imperialist expansion and retreat. And though the rejection of his program certainly bolstered the position of the broad, anti-imperialist Left, both major parties remained firmly in the hands of those the corporatists and militarists who had guided America since World War II, and it would thus be foolish of antiwar advocates to suppose that Watergate had truly opened the way for victory of the non-imperialist alternative. The post-Vietnam crisis was still in its early stages and the editors of *Ramparts* wondered about the future of American foreign policy now that Nixon seemed to be destroying the Republican Party. "We can be sure," the editors concluded, "that in its third century, America faced political turmoil the likes of which it had never experienced before.[170]

In October 1973, *Ramparts* published an essay titled "An Inside Look: Watergate and the World of the CIA," written by L. Fletcher Prouty, who was the Air Force officer in charge of Air Force support of the CIA, a position he held from 1955 to 1963. His office put him in constant contact with the top officers of the intelligence establishment, and he had traveled to more than forty countries at the CIA's behest. He was also one of the few people with inside knowledge of the CIA who was not required to take a lifetime oath of silence.

His book, *The Secret Team* (1973), was, Prouty wrote, as explosive as the Watergate revelations had been. And perhaps no disclosure in it had been more ominous than the 1970 Domestic Intelligence Plan authored by Tom Charles Huston. The plan provided for the use of electronic surveillance, mail coverage,

---

[170] *Ramparts* editorial Staff, "Watergate," *Ramparts Magazine*, August 1973, p. 35.

undercover agents and other measures to an extent unprecedented in domestic intelligence gathering. This program was to be directed by a committee of representatives from all of the national intelligence agencies. It went a long way toward justifying the worst paranoia Americans had felt during the previous quarter century over the growth of secrecy and deception in the U.S. Much of this anxiety was stoked by what Prouty referred to as the "CIA Mentality," the stealthy abuse of power and the practice of deception of the American public, all of which performed under the cloak of secrecy and often in the name of anticommunism and national security. In fact, what made the Watergate case different from other scandals was, Prouty explained, that the system and methods used, the means by which it was all planned, staffed with experts, financed clandestinely and carried out was all taken from the operating method of the CIA.[171]

---

[171] L. Fletcher Prouty, "An Inside Look: Watergate and the World of the CIA," *Ramparts Magazine*, October 1973, p. 21.

Prouty's essay was followed in the October 1973 edition of *Ramparts* by an investigative article titled "The Strange Tale of The Secret Army Organization (USA)," written by Richard Popkin, who taught philosophy at Washington University, St. Louis. Popkin was a world-renowned expert on skepticism and author of *The Second Oswald* (1966). Popkin argued that the Nixon administration's flirtation with the far right in the months before the 1972 Republican National Convention advanced the cause of terrorism. San Diego was supposed to be Richard Nixon's "Lucky City," a Navy town with a world-famous zoo and a new mayor named Pete Wilson. Local boosters saw the planned Republican convention as the biggest thing to happen to San Diego since the Pan-American Expo. Then suddenly, in May 1972, less than ninety days before the opening of the RNC, its Chair Bob Dole announced the convention would be relocating to Miami. At the time, the media pointed to two possible reasons for the party's sudden change of heart. One was the embarrassment caused by Dita Beard, an ITT lobbyist who had written a secret memo (leaked to Jack Anderson) that the way to get the Department of Justice to drop an antitrust investigation was for ITT to contribute $400,000 to the convention. San Diego's new ITT Sheraton was to be Nixon's headquarters during the convention. The other reason cited was fear that more than a quarter million young antiwar demonstrators would descend on the city when the Republicans arrived in August. Certainly those organizing the protests were confident that a combination of antiwar, anti-Nixon sentiment among young people combined with the lure of a summer week on the beaches of Southern California would guarantee a massive turnout. An internal Justice Department study claimed that the San Diego Police were not well trained in the handling of large demonstrations and predicted a high probability of violence.

Violence was, in fact, taking place months before the convention was scheduled to arrive, inspired both by an FBI directed right-wing terror network and Nixon's own White House Plumbers. In the 1960s, the Minutemen was a right-wing paramilitary outfit that believed the U.S. government had been overrun by communist infiltrators and that an underground patriot army had to be formed to fight a guerilla war against the reds. When they began to carry out bank robberies to finance their activities they were infiltrated and broken up by the FBI. In 1970, veterans of the Minutemen met secretly in Arizona to form a new paramilitary outfit called the Secret Army Organization. San Diego, which was home to some thirty members of the organization, soon emerged as the most active SAO chapter in the nation under the leadership of an unemployed contractor named Jerry Lynn Davis and a fireman named Howard Berry Godfrey.

Godfrey had also been working for the FBI as a Minuteman informant since 1967 when he had been arrested for brandishing a gun during a traffic dispute and possession of explosives the police found when they went to search his home. As a SAO State Commander he recruited new members from the Mormon church in which he and several of his FBI handlers were active. As the SAO's intelligence officer he also provided the terrorist group with FBI funds and information on San Diego's antiwar organizers. In late 1971 and early 1972, activists organizing protests at the upcoming Republican convention became the target of death threats, tear-gas attacks, vandalism and firebombings.

On the night of January 6, 1972, Godfrey and fellow SAO member George "Mickey" Hoover cruised past the home of one of the activists in the Ocean Beach section of the city. Hoover fired two shots from a stolen 9-millimeter pistol into the house, seriously wounding a young woman named Paula Tharp. The next day, Godfrey gave the weapon to his FBI control agent Steve Christiansen who hid it under his couch for the next six months. Meanwhile, the Republicans were getting nervous about the local intelligence they were receiving. On February 18, 1972, the day Nixon left for his historic trip to China, Godfrey published a poster of Nixon with a caption that read "Wanted for Treason" accusing the President and Secretary of State Henry Kissinger of conspiring with the Red Chinese to betray the U.S. The SAO distributed the poster in fifteen cities (the FBI reimbursed Godfrey for the printing costs).

The SAO which had by now begun warehousing rifles, mortar rounds, land-mines and explosives in garages around the city discussed how they might take turns mortaring the protesters outside and the Republicans inside the Convention Center. Meanwhile, White House plumber G. Gordon Liddy was simultaneously developing his own plans involving the kidnapping of antiwar leaders in San Diego. In May 1972, the Republican National Committee, worried about growing security issues, decided to hold the convention in Miami. A month later William Yakopec, a SAO member who had been recruited into the group by the FBI's Godfrey, bombed the Guild, a local porno theater. The bomb blew out the screen, scattering debris on theater patrons including a deputy city attorney and two vice cops. Soon, more than a dozen SAO members had been rounded up and jailed. At that point the SAO began plotting to assassinate San Diego's police chief, local Alcohol Tobacco and Firearm (ATF) agents, and other government officials they wrongly believed to be communists. Godfrey's testimony ultimately helped convict several of his confederates. Jerry Lynn Davis and other SAOers then began talking to local reporters about meetings at the "Gunsmoke Ranch," a shooting range outside San Diego, where Godfrey had introduced them to a man named Donald Simms, who Davis later identified as Donald Segretti, G. Gordon Liddy's White House operative. Segretti and the SAO apparently discussed plans to kidnap activists and take them to Mexico where they would be killed and their bodies dumped. The canceling of the RNC in San Diego in 1972 underscored the heinous nature of Nixon's diabolical use of his secret police force and the subsequent

weaponization of the American legal system.

CHAPTER TEN

"Executive Ineptitude and Corruption"

Though *Ramparts Magazine* tended to focus on issues often overlooked by the mainstream American corporate media, the magazine was also a kind of watchdog that soberly assessed some of the nation's most prominent political figures. *Ramparts* published several articles about prominent American political figures, particularly presidents and candidates for that position all through the 1960s and early 1970s, most notably Barry Goldwater, Lyndon Johnson, Ronald Reagan, and Richard Nixon, all of whom were prominently featured in the magazine.

In November 1964, days before the general election, *Ramparts* published a series of scathing essays depicting the Republican Party's nominee, Barry Goldwater, as a dangerous threat to the future of the United States and the rest of the world. The series was titled "The Compleat [sic] Goldwater" and included essays titled "The Literary Goldwater;" "The British Goldwater;"

"The German Goldwater;" "The Theatrical Goldwater;" "The Feiffer Goldwater;" "The Jewish Goldwater;" and "The Black Goldwater." None of which proffered anything even proximate to an endorsement of the candidate.

Maxwell Geismar argued in "The Literary Goldwater" that the senator from Arizona's ideas for the economy and foreign policy were "regressive" and what he proposed for American "national conduct" was "shocking, dangerous, and destructive." Goldwater, the author of *The Conscience Of A Conservative* (1960) was, Geismar asserted, "an inhuman egotist… Doctor Strangelove incarnate… paranoidal, utterly evil, and close to suicidal." Goldwater, Geismar concluded, represented the "spirit of McCarthyism, festering underground for so many years, and now revived and refurbished, adorned with white-collar respectability, but employing the same demonic viciousness beneath a calmer logic, and the same psychological tactics."[172]

Terence Prittie, the author of *Germans Against Hitler* (1964), was the chief diplomatic correspondent of *The Guardian* in London England during the 1964 general election. His essay, published in the November 1964 edition of *Ramparts,* was titled "The British Goldwater." In it Prittie expressed slightly less animus towards the author of *The Conscience Of A Conservative* as Geismar did. "In British eyes," Prittie wrote of Goldwater, the Republican candidate seemed to "exemplify rightwing radicalism" which was inimical, Prittie believed, to "democracy of the Western pattern" and who seemed to possess the character of men like Curtis Lemay, who viewed nuclear weapons as merely another weapon in a nation's arsenal and thus posed an existential threat to all of humanity.[173] In other words,

---

[172] Maxwell Geismar, "The Compleat Goldwater: The Literary Goldwater," *Ramparts Magazine*, November 1964, p. 12.

[173] Terence Prittie, "The Compleat Goldwater: The British Goldwater," *Ramparts Magazine*, November 1964, p. 20.

Geismar believed Goldwater to be a fascist at best and homicidal maniac at worst.

Neal Ascherson was a correspondent for *The London Observer*. His essay in the "Compleat Goldwater" series was titled "The German Goldwater." Ascherson argued that most Germans he spoke to about Goldwater feared that the radically conservative senator from Arizona would bring about another world war. Goldwater's loaded rhetoric about defeating "creeping socialism," Ascherson also noted, and Goldwater's supposed fondness for the John Birch Society earned the special interest of the neo-Nazis in Germany, many of whom admired the Republican candidate.

Sidney Michaels' essay was titled "The Theatrical Goldwater." He compared Goldwater's "contradictory" and "irresponsible" proposals intended as solutions to complex problems as being reminiscent of Hitler's reductionist rhetoric in the 1930s. But the most

---

important difference between Hitler and Goldwater, Michaels asserted, was that Hitler achieved election during the Great Depression, a time when starving and unemployed people were especially desperate for scapegoats to explain their plight, which made choosing a fanatic leader deplorable but not without logic. Goldwater, conversely, had moved to the mainstream of American politics at a time when some scholars conceived of the U.S. as being an "Affluent Society."

Jules Feiffer contributed a pictorial essay titled "The Feiffer Goldwater" that lampooned the radical Republican candidate's supporters as paranoid schizophrenics. Feiffer depicted Goldwater's base to be deplorables on the wrong side of history blindly following a mad man into an abyss.

Feiffer's pictorial essay was followed by an article contributed by Judd Teller, who was the author of *Scapegoat of Revolution: The Fate of the Jews in the Last Five Centuries* (1954). Teller argued that Jewish Americans seemed somewhat confused and mostly dismayed that one of the two major political parties in the U.S. not only failed to repudiate a rightwing fascism comparable to Hitlerism, but they nominated him to lead their party and ostensibly to lead the nation and free world in its fight against communism, which had long been associated amongst rightwing fascists such as Hitler and Mussolini to be closely associated to international communism. Many Israelis, Teller reminded readers, continued to live on a kibbutz in 1964.

The second-to-last essay in "The Compleat Goldwater" series was titled "The Black Goldwater," which was contributed by Louis E. Lomax, the author of *The Negro Revolt* (1962). "As a Christian-Humanist," Lomax wrote, "I view the Goldwater nomination as an insult." Lomax was particularly appalled by the Senator's frequent invoking of God's blessings upon Goldwaterism during his infamous acceptance speech at the 1964 Republican National Convention at the Cow Palace in Daly

City, California."[174] Lomax noted that Goldwater voted against the civil rights bill on constitutional grounds, but went on to say he felt that the bill's purpose was morally right, and that, in Lomax's words, the "Negro should, indeed, be given everything spelled out in the bill." And yet, Lomax lamented, "the white South loves Barry" due to the Senator's skillful use of racially coded language, such as advocating for "states' rights." Lomax presciently predicted that several Southern states, which were traditionally Dixiecrat, might likely shift into the Goldwater/Republican column because he was known as the candidate that was "against the coloreds" and an advocate of states' rights.[175]

The final article about Goldwater published in the November 1964 edition of *Ramparts* was titled "The McIntyre/Goldwater Axis," written by Edward M. Keating. *Ramparts*

---

[174] Louis E. Lomax, "The Black Goldwater," *Ramparts Magazine*, November 1964, p. 31.

[175] Ibid, p. 32.

was initially a Catholic magazine. Up until the time the publication moved its headquarters from suburban Southern California to metropolitan San Francisco, nearly each edition committed a great deal of ink to issues pertaining to the Church, which included being critical of the hypocrisy of Catholics. Such was the case with Keating's article. He argued that James Francis Aloysius McIntyre, who had been the archbishop of Los Angeles since 1948, was in many ways cut from the same spiritual and intellectual cloth as Goldwater. Both men, Keating argued, wanted Church and State to "be carried back to those tranquil days where six-guns and the Inquisition settled matters both quickly and unequivocally."[176]

In April 1965, four months after Goldwater's landslide loss to Lyndon Johnson, *Ramparts* published an essay titled "The Minority Mandate," written by Arthur I. Waskow. He

---

[176] Edward M. Keating, "The McIntyre/Goldwater Axis," *Ramparts Magazine*, November 1964, pp. 36-37, p. 37.

argued that Goldwater's defeat was a mandate against turning control of nuclear weapons over to generals in the field; it was a mandate against increasing the military budget and re-igniting the arms race; it was a mandate against using H-bombs in Vietnam; it was a mandate against letting Mississippi and Alabama "put the Negroes back in their place;" it was a mandate against filling American streets with policemen who could arrest on suspicion and convict with the third degree; it was a mandate against selling the Tennessee Valley Authority; it was a mandate against making Social Security voluntary. "In short," Waskow wrote, Goldwater's defeat was a mandate "against abolishing the world — literally, with H-bombs — and against abolishing the United States government—figuratively, with Congressional legislation."[177] Waskow, however, also noted that the U.S. polity was massive and diffuse and that

---

[177] Arthur I. Waskow, "The Minority Mandate," *Ramparts Magazine*, April 1965, p. 19.

the "minority mandate" that Goldwater represented was the antithesis of the majority mandate of 1964. He presciently noted that the extremism of the minority mandate could one day become the majority. Indeed, though Goldwater lost to Johnson in a route in the 1964 general election, the tide seemed to be turning more conservative in reaction to the civil rights movement and growing opposition to America's increased involvement in Indochina. The Deep South, for example, overwhelmingly supported Goldwater, who was a self-styled state's rights advocate, who many of the above essayists perceived to be a racist with fascist inclinations. Many of the essayists also noted the deep strain of racism and fascist tendencies deeply rooted on the American polity and identity that stretched all the way to the nation's founding as a bastion of slavery. Goldwater tapped into that strain in 1964, which established a blueprint for the "Southern Strategy," which helped turn the South into a Republican Stronghold by the time Richard Nixon resigned from office a decade

after Goldwater's defeat to Johnson.[178]
Goldwater's supporters and their "minority
mandate" seemed to foreshadow the rise of
neoconservatism in the waning decades of the
twentieth century by demanding that they had
established a new mandate to be championed by
the likes of Nixon, Ronald Reagan, and the Bush
Dynasty in subsequent decades.

The animus shifted significantly from
Goldwater to Johnson in subsequent editions of
Ramparts. In May 1965, for example, the editors
published an article titled "LBJ and the Politics of
Theology." The editors noted that Johnson's
attempt to alleviate the rapid overpopulation
rocking the Third World with birth control

---

[178] The Southern Strategy was a Republican Party
electoral strategy to increase political support among white
voters in the South by appealing to racism against African
Americans. As the civil rights movement and dismantling of
Jim Crow laws in the 1950s and 1960s visibly deepened
existing racial tensions in much of the Southern United States,
Republican politicians such as presidential candidates
Goldwater and then Nixon developed strategies that
successfully contributed to the political realignment of many
white, conservative voters in the South that had traditionally
supported the Democratic Party. It also helped push the
Republican Party much more to the right.

included in aid packages would put him at odds with the Catholic Church, who were an important voting bloc in the 1960s. Johnson feared losing Catholic voters, who prior to *Roe v. Wade* (1973), tended to vote for Democrats. The editorial underscored how the conservatism of American institutions hampered progressivism in the American polity and undercut social programs designed to alleviate the suffering of Catholics in the developing world, where the Church held enormous power and in many cases were at least partly responsible for the entrenched poverty and overpopulation that organizations such as the Peace Corps sought to address.

In August 1965, *Ramparts* published an editorial written soon after the March on Selma written by William Stringfellow titled "The Wagner-Wallace Syndrome." There was, Stringfellow argued, no significant ethical distinction between George Wallace, who was the white supremacist Governor of Alabama, and that of the Mayor of New York City in 1965,

Robert Wagner. Wagner's indifference to the inveterate racism in the South and Northern cities alike was, Stringfellow asserted, "the moral equivalent of Wallace's impudence." Both men were also, Stringfellow wrote, "intransigent toward change in the status quo."[179] But, Stringfellow predicted, Selma would prove to be a watershed moment amongst white folks all across the U.S. Selma would be, he prophesied, "represent the moment when legions of contented and prosperous white people would begin at last to comprehend what had been happening to the nation and how the nation could be destroyed by its hypocrisy and racism."[180]

In November 1965, *Ramparts* published an essay contributed by Jessica Mitford, who was the author of the bestselling expose titled *The American Way of Death* (1963), which examined what a boondoggle the funeral director industry

---

[179] William Stringfellow, "Editorial: The Wagner-Wallace Syndrome," *Ramparts Magazine*, August 1965, p. 8.

[180] Ibid, p. 10.

in the U.S. was. Mitford's essay was titled "The Rest of Ronald Reagan." Reagan was running for governor of California, which Mitford depicted as just another role he was playing. The article consisted of a cartoon version of Reagan dressed in a number of costumes including a swimsuit, Lion's suit, and a football uniform circa the 1930s. She also illuminated that American politics in the 1960s was fast becoming little more than a television production readymade for the unthinking masses, and candidates as products to be sold and consumed like Life Cereal. "Who will Central Casting pick as his running mate?" she sardonically and rhetorically queried readers.[181]

The California milieu that gave rise to Richard Nixon and Ronald Reagan was also prominently depicted and lampooned in the October 1966 edition of *Ramparts* in an essay titled "Golly Gee, California is a Strange Place." The editors pointed out that Governor Pat Brown

---

[181] Jessica Mitford, "The Rest of Ronald Reagan," *Ramparts Magazine*, November 1965, p. 36.

had a Mickey Mouse-type quality. Both the governor and the mascot of Disneyland had, for example, a penchant for saying "golly gee." Brown in particular, the editors believed, had failed miserably as a leader during his tenure, which set the stage for Reagan's political ascendance. Section III of the editorial was titled "The Creation of Ronald Reagan," whose political rise was, the editors argued, as much the product of "the failure of the liberal nerve" in California as it was Reagan's phony folksy charm.[182]

One particular area that the editors felt that Brown had failed was in regard to the failed Water Plan. The economic expansion following World War II lured millions of newcomers to California. Rapid population growth, much of which was fueled by post-war America's Sunbelt militarization, along with the state's cyclical

---

[182] *Ramparts* editorial staff, "Golly Gee, California is a Strange Place," *Ramparts Magazine*, October 1966, pp. 11-33.

droughts, severely strained California's water resources, especially in dry Southern California, which inspired the proposal for the California State Water Project. The objective of the project was to address the fact that one half of the state's people lived in a region containing one percent of the state's natural supply of water. Much of the state's extant water was controlled by regional bodies, and the federal government. These federally controlled areas were under the jurisdiction of the Bureau of Reclamation, which in the mid-1960s, was considering the implementation of a 160-acre principle designed to limit delivery of federally subsidized water to parcels equal to the size of a homestead, which was 160 acres.

This stoked strong opposition from the agricultural industry because it would require significant splintering of existent land holdings. To relieve this threat to the agricultural economy, Brown and other state leaders began the State Water Project, whose master plan included a vast system of reservoirs, aqueducts, and pipelines powered by pump stations and electrical generating plants to transport the water statewide. This included the capture of the Sacramento River runoff, redirecting the sea bound water through the San Joaquin Valley, which not only irrigated the arid desert regions, but also provided Southern California, particularly Los Angeles County, with the water required to sustain expansions in population and industry. The entire project was expected to take sixty years to finish, costing a total $13 billion. But Brown ultimately caved into the big agricultural interests and lobbied Congress to exempt California from the 160-acre rule, lauding the benefit of employment and progress to the state's northern and southern residents, and calling for an end to the north-south rivalry.

Another way Brown, the editors argued, "lost his nerve" as a leader during his governorship was in regard to his handling of the Caryl Chessman appeal. Chessman was a convicted robber, kidnapper and rapist who was sentenced to death for a series of crimes committed in January 1948 in the Los Angeles area. The "first modern American executed for a non-lethal kidnapping," Chessman was convicted under a loosely interpreted "Little Lindbergh Law" – which was later repealed, but not retroactively – that defined kidnapping as a capital offense under certain circumstances. Chessman's case attracted worldwide attention, and helped propel the movement to end the use of capital punishment in the state of California. While in prison Chessman wrote four books, including a memoir.

His books and the public campaign to free him ignited a worldwide movement to spare his life, while focusing attention on the larger question of the death penalty in the U.S. at a time when most Western countries had abandoned it, or were in the process of doing so. Brown was flooded with letters pleading for Chessman's clemency from the likes of Eleanor Roosevelt and Billy Graham. The Chessman affair put Brown, who was an opponent of the death penalty, in a difficult and precarious position. He was unable to grant Chessman executive clemency because the California Constitution required the commutation of a two-time felon's death sentence to be ratified by the California Supreme Court, which declined ratification by a vote of 4-3. After a long period of inaction Brown finally issued a 60-day stay of execution on February 19, 1960. He issued the stay, he said, out of concern that the execution could threaten the safety of Dwight Eisenhower during the President's visit to South America, due to the fact that the Chessman case had inflamed anti-American sentiment around the world. Chessman's stay of execution, along with his last appeals, ran out in April 1960, and he finally went to the gas chamber at San Quentin Prison on May 2 of that year.

Brown's popularity, however, flagged especially amongst California's liberals amidst the Free Speech Movement in 1964 at the University of California at Berkeley. Brown seemed to side with Clark Kerr and the police against the student-protestors. All this, *Ramparts* editors argued, set the stage for Reagan to rule what they referred to as "Tomorrowland." Reagan's popularity was, the editors explained, due largely to the fact that he was a caricature that represented escapism rather than truth or reality. Californians in 1966 were, the editors wrote, "restless" because they could not control their environment and because "their social fantasies" clashed "with the realities of Watts and because their sense of United States power" clashed "with the reality of Vietnam."[183] Brown's losing bid for a third term to Reagan a month after *Ramparts* published the editorial forever shaped not only California's history, but also the fate of the U.S., considering Brown's defeat ultimately helped pave the way for Reagan's path the White House, and Jerry Brown's path to the governor's mansion in 1974.

"Golly Gee, California is a Strange Place" was followed in the October 1966 edition of *Ramparts* by a pictorial essay titled "Ronnie for

---

[183] Ibid, p. 28.

Governor?" contributed by Bob Abel and Dick Guindon. The essay, like Mitford's, depicted Reagan playing a number of roles, including "The Gipper" in *Knut Rockne, All American* (1940). "Ronnie For Governor?" underscored that Reagan was primed to play his greatest role yet, at least until the 1980s.

In January 1967, *Ramparts* published a positive review of Rowland Evans and Robert D. Novak's recently published *Lyndon B. Johnson: The Exercise of Power* (1966) written by Adam Hochschild titled "The Emperor's Court." The book examined Johnson's pursuit of power beginning as a senator in 1953 up to 1966, and chronicled the sorted cast of characters who helped pave Johnson's ascendance, including two corrupt construction magnates in the state of Texas who held heavy sway in state politics and had ties to the mafia.

In February 1967, *Ramparts* published a profile titled "A Political Portrait of Robert Kennedy," written by Robert Scheer, which was by no means an endorsement of John Kennedy's younger brother, who had not even declared his candidacy. Kennedy's program for America, Scheer explained, differed in no essential or significant way from that of Johnson's or any other mainstream politician. He shared the prevailing view of the Cold War and the benevolent workings of modern capitalism, and very carefully avoided any fundamental criticism of either. In his reliance on private investment as a panacea for the ills of American ghettos and underdeveloped countries alike, he was also, Scheer warned readers, clearly to the right of the New Deal.

Kennedy had, Scheer explained, also been unwilling to deal with the problem of the U.S.'s massive military industrial complex or propose any plans for the conversion from a war economy to a peacetime one. For all the zest of the Kennedy men, Scheer lamented, they had retained a conservative approach to issues, having carefully cultivated an aura of youth as an alternative to political integrity and commitment. It was a stance, Scheer explained, that provided the illusion of change without its troublesome substance. Robert Kennedy's favorite phrase, Scheer wrote, was the one from his brother's campaign which promised to "get the country moving again." But where, Scheer wondered, did Bobby Kennedy want to take the country?[184]

In March 1968, soon after Eugene McCarthy had entered the Democratic Primary race, Andrew Kopkind contributed an article to *Ramparts* titled "The McCarthy Campaign," which described the candidate as lacking a coherent platform and strategy to win. McCarthy was however, Kopkind hailed, backed by a ragtag collective that hated America's war in Vietnam and were terrified by the failure of the institutions they had once relied on. They would not think, Kopkind explained, of voting for the incumbent Johnson, nor could they bring themselves to vote for Bobby Kennedy; they were, Kopkind wrote, made physically ill by the

---

[184] Robert Scheer, "A Political Portrait of Robert Kennedy," *Ramparts Magazine*, February 1967, p. 17.

sight of Nixon and the thought of Reagan. And though they were antiwar, they were not the kind of folks to march on the Pentagon. Liberals' last, best hope was McCarthy, Kopkind concluded, but the problem was, McCarthy could not even tell his supporters what his campaign was all about.[185]

In May 1968, soon after Johnson shocked the nation by declaring that he would not seek reelection, *Ramparts* published a pictorial editorial titled "As We Saw Him" that lampooned the lame duck president as a cartoon cowboy made of papier-mâché with a vulture-like nose. The article seemed to revel in Johnson's swift and cataclysmic collapse.

"As We Saw Him" was followed in the May 1968 edition of *Ramparts* by another essay contributed by Scheer titled "The 'Peace' Candidates." Both Robert Kennedy and Eugene McCarthy, Scheer wrote, had generally succeeded in projecting stylistic alternatives to

---

[185] Andrew Kopkind. "The McCarthy Campaign," *Ramparts Magazine*, March 1968, p. 55.

the Johnson administration, but without making a comparable break with its basic content. Failing to develop programmatic and institutional alternatives rather than personal and marginal criticism of the Johnson administration, Scheer concluded, both "peace" candidates would inevitably end up with the same policies and the same disasters as their predecessor.[186]

In late-October, a week before the 1968 general election, *Ramparts* published an essay titled "Travels With the Right: Wallace" written by Pete Hamill, who had been on the campaign trail with Alabama Governor George Wallace – the unabashedly white supremacist third party candidate who was running against the Democratic nominee, Hubert Humphrey, and the Republican nominee, Richard Nixon. Hamill expressed trepidation that the election would usher in a resurgent conservatism championed by scared Americans "lusting for some terrible vengeance, some bloody catharsis that would

---

[186] Robert Scheer, "The 'Peace' Candidates," *Ramparts Magazine*, May 1968, p. 63

make everything the way they think it once was in this country." Wallace was not, Hamill asserted, the cause of spiritual disease that existed in the American polity, he was but a symptom.[187] The disease was, Hamill concluded, fear.

Ramparts published an editorial days after Nixon's triumph titled simply as "Nixon." The editorial depicted a cartoon drawing of Nixon wearing a King's crown. The editors described Nixon as "a man with no beliefs, no private life of any mystery or gaudiness," a man who was "beyond roots, beyond true passion, a convenient cipher." He was, they concluded, the best symbol America possessed of all the terrible things that had happened to the U.S. in the years since John F. Kennedy was murdered. "We have," the editors wrote, "passed so much time in the company of hate, we have committed so many foul and unholy acts, that as a nation we

---

[187] Pete Hamill, "Travels With the Right: Wallace," *Ramparts Magazine*, October 26, 1968, pp. 48.

no longer care what anyone else thinks about us. We are at last shameless and alone like Richard Nixon."[188] This editorial was immediately followed by an editorial titled "Humphrey" that included a cartoon of Nixon's defeated opponent as Humpty Dumpty teetering atop a brick wall.

In December 1968, *Ramparts* published an essay titled "Infiltrating Nixon," contributed by Emma Rothschild, who had been embedded with the "Nixon Girls" in the days leading up to the general election. Nixon Girls were, Rothschild explained, comparable to the Dallas Cowboy Cheerleaders. But rather than cheering on that American-football team, they advocated the candidate they seemed to unabashedly adore as America's savior from the unrest that defined the Sixties. Rothschild wrote that, "The Nixon Girls served as an example of how inflatable, vapid, hollow, and shameless the Nixon campaign appeared to be to many liberals vacuous Nixon's supporters were.

---

[188] *Ramparts* editorial staff, "Nixon," *Ramparts Magazine*, November 17, 1968, p. 40.

In August 1969, *Ramparts* published an essay about Nixon's recently confirmed cabinet, which included Clifford Hardin, Robert Finch, and Walter Hickel, to name a few. They were, as was Nixon as depicted as a king, portrayed as cartoons. That article was followed by an essay titled "Rocky Takes a Trip," written by David Horowitz. In 1964 Nelson Rockefeller fell shy of the Republican Party's nomination as its presidential nominee to Goldwater. But Rockefeller, as governor of the state of New York until 1973, remained an important operator in the American economy and political system. Latin America, Horowitz argued, functioned generally as a source of fabulous wealth for giant U.S. corporate interests, and for the Rockefeller family and empire in particular. He noted the Rockefeller's oil interests in Venezuela – the world's largest exporter and third largest producer of oil (behind the U.S. and the USSR). Oil accounted for ninety-three percent of Venezuela's export earnings and sixty-three percent of government revenue. Poverty was, however, widespread in Venezuela in large part, Horowitz noted, as a direct result of this expansion and its consequences, which included billions in repatriated profits escaping into U.S. coffers. Poverty would worsen in Latin America, Horowitz speculated, as long as the policy of the most powerful nations was dictated by the policies of business. The elimination of Latin American poverty, Horowitz concluded, could not happen by way of the Alliance for Progress type of reform programs under the aegis of the same financiers and imperialists, such as Rockefeller, who were responsible for the system and received its maximum benefits.[189]

In September 1969, *Ramparts* published an essay titled "Mr. Rockefeller Builds his Dream House," which was contributed by W. David Gardner. Gardner wrote of a recent shopping mall that had been built in Albany, New York – the state capital. It seemed, Gardner noted, that everyone would get a piece of the pie as a result

---

[189] David Horowitz, "Rocky Takes a Trip," *Ramparts Magazine*, August 1969, p. 61.

of this newly conceived Mecca of consumer convenience. The smart real estate operators would "make their killing," Gardner explained, "the local political fiefdom would fill its coffers; the bankers would juggle their hundreds of millions in tax-free bond interest; the State Department of Health would have its 640-foot ventilation shaft; and Nelson Rockefeller would have his monument to mass consumption." And after the mall was completed, Gardner concluded, and the pie was all sliced up, the poor blacks who used to live there, having been largely barred from the construction work itself — would be invited back to work in the service industry for low wage jobs that lacked benefits and security.[190]

In October 1969, *Ramparts* published an article titled "Barry Goldwater: An Open Letter to my Friend," written by Karl Hess, who was a former editor of *Newsweek*. Hess was also the principal author of the 1960 Republican platform,

---

[190] W. David Gardner, "Mr. Rockefeller Builds his Dream House," *Ramparts Magazine*, September 1969, p. 39.

a co-author of the 1964 platform, and Goldwater's chief speech writer in the lead up to the 1964 general election. In 1969, Hess was moonlighting as a newly devout participant in the New Left and thus penned an open letter to Goldwater making the case that his friend should get on the right side of history by joining the New Left, which Hess perceived to be, like he was, a decentralist. "There was also, Hess believed, something very attractive in the New Left's analysis of the American corporate system and its use of political power to preserve and enlarge itself," he wrote to Goldwater about the appeal of the New Left.[191]

In September 1970, *Ramparts* editorial staff published a piece titled "Lenin, Trotsky, Rockefeller and Stalin." In 1932 Mexican artist Diego Rivera had been hired to paint a mural in the lobby of the recently completed Rockefeller Center in midtown Manhattan, which had been

---

[191] Karl Hess, "Barry Goldwater: An Open Letter to my Friend," *Ramparts Magazine*, October 1969, p. 28.

built as a monument to American power, prestige, capitalism, and wealth. The young and up-and-coming Nelson Rockefeller, who was just twenty-four years old, but already a trustee of the Museum of Modern Art and the Metropolitan Museum. He hired Rivera to paint a 17 x 63-foot fresco in the lobby of the Center's main building. To Rockefeller's consternation, however, Rivera placed the unmistakable figure of Vladimir Lenin in the middle of the mural. Rockefeller fired off a note to the artist demanding that Lenin be removed from the mural. Rivera refused, and after much diplomatic maneuvering, Rockefeller sent an agent to pay the artist off and to fire him. Rockefeller had the fresco destroyed. Rockefeller was, somewhat ironically, made president of the Museum of Modern Art in 1939. The anecdote about Rockefeller and Rivera was followed immediately in the September 1970 edition of *Ramparts* by E.B. White's poem inspired by the conflict between Rockefeller and Rivera titled, "I Paint What I see, A Ballad of Artistic Integrity."

In January 1972, in the midst of primary season, *Ramparts* published a profile written by Frank Browning titled "Senator 'Scoop' Jackson: Pentagon Populist." Jackson was a prototypical Cold War American liberal – a supporter of social welfare programs associated with Johnson's Great Society, but also a communist hardliner who advocated an increasingly militarized American society. Jackson, who despite his support of civil rights programs, was a staunch opponent of labor unions, and was not well known nationally when he first announced his candidacy for President of the United States in January of 1972. McGovern, who eventually won the Democratic Party's nomination, accused Jackson of racism for his opposition to busing despite Jackson's longstanding record on civil rights issues. Jackson's highpoint in the campaign was a distant third in the early Florida primary, but he failed to stand out of the pack of better-known rivals, and he made real news only later in the campaign, as part of the "Stop McGovern" coalition, which cast McGovern as a champion of "Acid, Amnesty (for men who had avoided the Draft) and Abortion." Jackson suspended active campaigning in May after a weak showing in the Ohio primary and finishing well behind McGovern, Ed Muskie, George Wallace, and Hubert Humphrey.

In June 1972, *Ramparts* provided candidates including Shirley Chisholm,[192] Hubert Humphrey, Ed Muskie, and George McGovern a platform to express their policy ideas based on questions posed by David Kolodney. Those questions included:

1. Shall the United States permanently withdraw all its armed forces (soldiers, sailors and airmen) from Vietnam on the sole condition of an agreement for the repatriation of prisoners of war, timed to coincide with our withdrawal?

---

[192] In 1968 Chisholm became the first African-American woman elected to the U.S. Congress. In 1972, she became the first black candidate for a major party's nomination for U.S. President and the first woman to run for the Democratic Party's presidential nomination.

2. Shall the U.S. similarly withdraw its armed forces from all of Indochina on the same single condition? What about U.S. bases in Thailand?

3. Shall the U.S. end all military aid to the Saigon regime (whether or not President Thieu should resign) on the same basis?

4. Shall the United States end all economic aid to the Saigon regime on the same basis (with any humanitarian exceptions such as an imported rice dole to be distributed through an agency)?

5. Shall the U.S. set a date by which it will carry out its withdrawal (as specified in the preceding answers) on the same single condition of an agreement on repatriation of POWs?

6. What date?[193]

---

[193] David Kolodney, "Electoral Politics: The Candidates Reply

Humphrey's responses were the most terse and uninspired. Muskie's were the most longwinded. Chisholm's were the most thoughtful and cogent. McGovern, however, ultimately won the nomination and lost the general election in a historic rout to Richard Nixon.

In September 1972, *Ramparts* published another essay penned by Kolodney soon after McGovern sealed the DNC's nomination titled "McGovern and the Left: Time for a Stand." Kolodney lamented that McGovern would need Chicago Mayor Richard Daley's support to win Illinois, which he would need to do to stand any chance against the incumbent Nixon. The irony of the New Left needing the support of Daley inspired creative and perhaps desperate thinking. McGovern's strategists hoped to register millions of new voters through the efforts of 100,000 registrar volunteers. Lacking the traditional big money sources, they talked of having a million contributors donate $25 each. Their aim was to arouse and energize, to activate and intensify support for their candidate. Nixon, however, ultimately won in a historic landslide. McGovern's defeat was a serious blow to the antiwar movement, which provided the various factions of the New Left some semblance of coherence.

"McGovern and the Left: Time for a Stand" was immediately followed in the September 1972 edition of *Ramparts* by an optimistic essay titled "The Democrats: A Winning Strategy," written by Jim Ridgeway. He proscribed ways in which the Democrats could win California, Texas, Illinois, Ohio, Michigan, and New Jersey, and potentially the general election. In hindsight, considering Nixon's resounding victory, Ridgeway's article seemed somewhat utopian, if not entirely delusional.

"McGovern and the Left: Time for a Stand" was followed in the September 1972 edition of *Ramparts* by an article titled "Richard Plays Realtor in San Clemente," written by Robert Fitch. The story chronicled Nixon's summer home, which was nestled on California's Pacific Coast – on two of the state's best surf breaks – Cotton Point and the Trestles. Nixon wanted to close that beach due to his fear of a security threat. This, however, potentially threatened to upset many Californians who could potentially pull their support from Nixon due to his plan to privatize one the state's most popular recreation destinations. Nixon ultimately found a compromise by making the beach adjacent to his property private concomitant to opening a new public beach six miles away from the "Summer White House" on Camp Pendleton Property. Nixon shrewdly spun the event as him being a champion Californians by taking a piece of land that was predominately used by the Marine's "top brass" and Southern California elites such as *The Los Angeles Times'* owner Otis Chandler, and gifted the beach to the people of California.

In October 1972, *Ramparts* published an essay titled "Oh, Sarge? He's a Good Soldier," written by Ridgeway about Sergeant Shriver, who had recently been named McGovern's running-mate. This coupling seemed odd to

Ridgeway considering that as the former Director of the Office of Economic Opportunity, the Democratic vice-presidential candidate had been the architect and administrator of many of the very same domestic policies and social programs McGovern had pledged to change or abolish.

In January 1973, two months after Nixon's defeat of McGovern, *Ramparts* published an essay titled "Who Really Lost the Election?" written by Bo Burlingham. Nixon's landslide victory in November 1972 had, Burlingham asserted, shattered any illusion that Americans were a compassionate people. But rather than Nixon winning the election, he found more fault in liberals and leftists for losing the election. He expressed deep regret that just forty-five percent of the eligible voters went to the polls, which he noted, was an important indicator of McGovern's failure. Second, Nixon's victory was built on a farcical illusion. "The 1960s was not a bad dream," Burlingham wrote. "The malcontents" would not go away, and the country could not be violently wrenched back into a Norman Rockwell fantasy."[194] Burlingham, however, failed to see that the illusion of a better yesterday being the future of America would endure in American politics for generations.

In January 1973, *Ramparts* published an essay titled "The Selling Out of the Candidate: 1972," contributed by Tom Oliphant, who was a member of *The Boston Globe's* Washington Bureau. Oliphant had covered McGovern's post-convention campaign between September - November 1972. Despite the title of the essay, Oliphant was actually quite sympathetic to McGovern who many had perceived as rhetorically back-peddling from his ideals in the run-up to the election in the hopes of defeating the incumbent. Oliphant, conversely, reminded readers of just how brazen, bold, and courageous McGovern had actually been at times.

McGovern, Oliphant argued, was a genuine progressive in stark contrast to Nixon

---

[194] Bo Burlingham, "Who Really Lost the Election?" *Ramparts Magazine*, January 1973, p. 9.

and most of the rest of Washington, which had, by the early 1970s, increasingly been associated with war, scandal, and corruption, including corruption of the Constitution by assaults on freedom of the press as well as the corruption of the American tax code via loopholes for a wealthy few, and most especially the corruption of the American political process by wanton attempts by the Nixon administration to bend the justice system to its will. The system could have been significantly changed for the better, Oliphant concluded, had Nixon been defeated by McGovern. And in the final analysis, McGovern's defeat was, Oliphant asserted, the defeat of the American people writ large. As such, it was imperative for the scores of voters who did not turn out in November of 1972, Oliphant concluded, to recognize the power they let slip through their hands and how catastrophic it could soon prove to be.

Lyndon Johnson died in January 1973 at the age of 64. In April 1973, *Ramparts* published an unsentimental obituary titled "LBJ: The Last

Roundup, A Post-Mortem," contributed by Andrew Kopkind. Kopkind lamented that the death of an American president gave Americans "nostalgic amnesia." Lyndon Johnson, who Kopkind described as a "madman, war maker, racist and cowboy" was oddly praised in numerous publications for, as Kopkind sardonically summarized, "letting us reason together, for sparing certain areas of Indochina from his airplanes and his bombs, for signing an anachronistic civil rights bill, and for hanging up his coonskin cap when the cow-poking got tough."[195] Kopkind could not quite conceive why people from so many political positions remembered Johnson's "craziness, his crassness, his malevolent machismo" as being "so charming, so entertaining," and adorable. "I'll always remember LBJ as a demented half-drunk mockery of manliness," Kopkind sneered, "a dirty young, middle-aged and old man who called in secretaries to give him head and

---

[195] Andrew Kopkind, "LBJ: The Last Roundup: A Post-Mortem," *Ramparts Magazine*, April 1973, p. 10.

generals to give him body-counts with equal relish, while mind-bent America lied to itself about him and watched the world go by."[196]

In October 1974, *Ramparts* published an essay titled "Gerald Ford, Understudy for Defeat," written by Kolodney. Ford seemed to Kolodney to be getting a free pass by the mainstream American Press such as *CBS* and *The New York Times*, both of which seemed eager to put the turmoil and divisions of the civil rights movement, Vietnam War Era, and Watergate behind the nation. *Ramparts*, however, noted that Ford was not even qualified for the job he accidently fell into, noting that he had not been elected as either vice president (he was appointed after Spiro Agnew was compelled to resign due to a financial scandal) or as president, the position of which he assumed after Nixon had resigned in the wake of the Watergate scandal and Constitutional Crisis he had created. Ford was thus an "accidental president" who

---

[196] Ibid, p. 13.

had not been selected by the American people, but by the disgraced Nixon. "The era of good feeling" that Ford supposedly represented was thus "a lie," Kolodney wrote, "and the honeymoon should never have begun."[197]

In April and July 1975, *Ramparts* published two articles titled "California Politics: The Riddle of Gov. Jerry Brown," contributed by Francis Carney, who was a professor of political science at the University of California at Riverside. The first essay in the series focused on the new Brown administration in California, particularly the "unusual character of the Governor and his appointees."[198] Carney noted how odd it seemed that Brown's rhetoric of fiscal responsibility echoed the rhetoric of Governor Reagan before him, which Carney believed harmed California's most vulnerable citizens. The second article, subtitled "The Policies,"

---

[197] David Kolodney, "Gerald Ford, Understudy for Defeat," *Ramparts Magazine*, October 1974, p. 17.

[198] Francis Carney, "California Politics: The Riddle of Gov. Jerry Brown," *Ramparts Magazine*, April 1975, p. 34.

assessed Brown's programs and their prospective significance for the state and the nation. Brown ultimately won the governorship of California and proved to be even more fiscally conservative than Reagan. He also ran for President of the United States in 1976 and was officially nominated at the 1976 DNC convention by the United Farm Worker's Cesar Chavez. Brown, however, lost the nomination to Carter, which was an indication of the growing significance of the Deep South in American politics.

Ramparts' essays about some of America's most prominent political figures and operatives served as a kind of metaphorical depiction for how culturally corrupt the nation was as a result of inveterate racism and as a bastion of rapacious capitalism, which had subsumed the American polity, which led to horror shows such as America's war in Vietnam and Watergate. As the next chapter helps to illuminate, Watergate was but one of many political scandals and corruption, which the editors of *Ramparts* believed to be endemic to the American polity during the 1960s and 1970s.

CHAPTER ELEVEN

"The Kennedys and the Warren Commission"

The editors at *Ramparts Magazine* were quite adamant that Americans had a right to know who killed the President of the United States and why. Several stories were published in the magazine that expressed grave doubt and regret about the rush to judgment in the Warren Commission, which was published less than a year after Kennedy's death. The Warren Commission determined that Lee Harvey Oswald was a lone gunman and not part of a larger conspiracy, which many considered an unsatisfactory, if not sinister, dissembling of the truth. *Ramparts* thus published scores of essays questioning the validity of the Warren Report that suggested that the death of the president was part of a grand conspiracy.

In November 1966, three years after Kennedy's murder, *Ramparts* published two editorials titled "In The Shadow of Dallas." In it the editors, who argued that the Warren Commission should have remained in existence for at least five years, questioned the validity of many of the Warren Commission's conclusions. When the Commission made its Report and disbanded, the editors felt it should be reopened. The first such essay was an editorial contributed by Penn Jones Jr., who was the author of the not yet published *Forgive My Grief: A Critical View of the Warren Commission Report on the Assassination of President John F. Kennedy* (1967). Jones described the goal of his article as an attempt to bring into some intelligible whole all the events surrounding the assassination of John F. Kennedy. He noted that many persons who were related to the tragedy in Dallas had gone missing, were murdered, or "met with death strangely." Despite the seeming danger of having knowledge of the events surrounding Kennedy's murder in Dallas, Jones wrote that he expected to work on the assassination for the rest of his life. He also predicted that no action would be taken by the government to sufficiently solve the crime. He, however, hoped that historians would one day be able to "point a more accurate finger."[199] And after spending several thousand hours knocking on doors, asking questions, concomitant to reading the Report, Jones believed audacious actions were taken by the Commission lawyers and the Chairman to obfuscate the evidence left after Kennedy, J.D. Tippit, and Oswald were killed. "The fanciful legend Earl Warren," Jones wrote, "helped to fix in the minds of Americans was the burden he must bear." Jones also assailed what he referred to as "timid liberals in Dallas" who also shared with Warren a great part of the responsibility for the pre-assassination attitudes in Dallas that permitted such an atmosphere to fester there. Liberals in Dallas did not work to make sure all facts were reported after the assassination either, Jones asserted, and this criminal neglect would, he assured readers, "blacken the name of Dallas for all time." Jones also cited the "the Jarnagin Report," in which a lawyer testified that Jack

---

[199] Penn Jones Jr., "In the Shadow of Dallas," *Ramparts Magazine*, November 1966, p. 31.

Ruby and Lee Harvey Oswald had been acquainted. Jones ominously concluded his essay by predicting that more killings were going to be necessary in order to keep the "crime of the century" hushed.[200]

Jones' editorial was followed in the series by an editorial written by David Welch titled "The Legacy of Penn Jones Jr." Jones' legacy was that an army of independent sleuths who were motivated by anything from an affection for President Kennedy to a plain zeal for truth, affiliated only in the most informal way, had, Welch wrote, become "the embodiment" of what was "finest in the American tradition, and a living indictment of government-by-closed-shop."[201] Welch admitted that at first he had refused to take the sleuths seriously. Then the editors at *Ramparts* reviewed their work and realized that they were doing the job the Dallas

---

[200] Ibid, p. 38.

[201] David Welsh, "In the Shadow of Dallas," *Ramparts Magazine*, November 1966, p. 39.

police, the Federal Bureau of Investigation, and the Warren Commission should have done in the first place.

And if many others, Welch asserted, treated these amateur investigators as some unique breed of kook, the Dallas police also took them seriously. When Shirley Martin, a housewife from Hominy, Oklahoma, made trips to Dallas to interview witnesses, the police tailed her, openly following her car at short distance, and stayed in her shadow until she left town. The FBI also took another one of the "sleuths" seriously enough to tap his phone. Two San Francisco sleuths also reported that their mail was habitually opened before it reached their door. Such intimidation, Welch wrote, had become so common that the sleuths hardly talked about it anymore.[202]

Welch then went on to describe the "Kennedy Curse" and listed a number of people

---

[202] Ibid, p. 39.

who allegedly had knowledge of the conspiracy who were killed in the three years since November 22, 1963. Marrs' also later provided an updated and extensive list of the "Kennedy Curse" in his book *Crossfire* (1989), which became the inspiration for Oliver Stone's *JFK* (1991). Welch further noted that Dallas Police Officer J.D. Tippit, who was allegedly shot by Oswald in a movie theater soon after Kennedy was shot, was never "conclusively" solved by the Warren Commission. He also asserted that the evidence in the report indicated that Bullet 399, which later became known as the "magic bullet," could not have caused all of Governor John Connally's wounds. Connally was in the seat ahead of Kennedy, who was in the back seat of the convertible with his wife, Jackie. One thing was clear, Welch asserted: that someone had better re-examine the "superbullet" theory, and consider the possibility that Bullet 399 — the only assassination bullet that had been ballistically matched to Oswald's rifle — was a plant.[203]

Despite his obvious anger and despair, Welch praised Jones and the small cadre of passionate and dedicated "sleuths" who had marshaled an impressive body of evidence to show that the Commission "solved" neither the assassination of Kennedy nor the murder of Tippit. This cadre of intrepid truth seekers who Welch believed were risking their lives by investigating had, he hailed, exposed the Commission's "religious determination" not to track down leads pointing to other possible assassins and cop killers. And they had shown how the time limit given by President Lyndon Johnson to the shorthanded Commission — before the 1964 elections — meant the investigation could only be a frivolous one. The so called Warren Commission, Welch concluded, was appointed by Lyndon Johnson, was responsible to Johnson, and respected a lawyer-

---

[203] Ibid, p. 49.

client relationship with Johnson. It was in that sense truly "the President's Commission."[204] In other words, Johnson was, Welch insinuated, the primary suspect in the alleged cover up.

In January 1967, *Ramparts* published a special report written by Welch and David Lifton titled "The Case for Three Assassins." They presented the case that no less than three gunmen fired on the Presidential motorcade in Dallas on November 22, 1963. Their conclusion had been reached following a ten-month investigation into the assassination of President Kennedy. Defenders of the Warren Commission had continually challenged its critics to come up with a more conclusive theory; Welch and Lifton believed that their special report did just that. They argued that the evidence indicated that since Kennedy's head jutted sharply to the back and to the left that he had to have also been shot from the right and by someone at ground level who was ahead of the motorcade on the grassy

---

[204] Ibid, p. 50.

knoll. There were, they noted, sixty-four witnesses that indicated that shots had been fired from the grassy knoll. Welch and Lifton also noted that Kennedy had been wounded in the throat, which, they asserted, was not possible unless there was a shooter other than Oswald, who was allegedly on the sixth floor of the book depository behind the motorcade. "How could the President have been shot in the front from the back?" Welch and Lifton demanded.[205]

In February 1967, a month after Jack Ruby died of cancer, *Ramparts* published "A Letter from Jail," written by Ruby, with a preface written Welch, who explained that the magazine decided to publish the letter, which he described as an "intriguing historical document," which he hoped might provide some insight into Ruby's mind during his time in jail. The *Ramparts* editorial staff, Welch stipulated, did not endorse any of the statements made in Ruby's letter,

---

[205] David Welsh and David Lifton, "The Case for Three Assassins," *Ramparts Magazine*, January 1967, p. 78.

many of which were demonstrably inaccurate and untrue. Most of the names mentioned in the letter had also been redacted in order to avoid injury to the persons named. The letter published by *Ramparts* was one of two unsigned letters, handwritten in pencil on slips from a memo pad, confiscated by one of Ruby's guards and subsequently smuggled from the jail. They were sold at auction in the Astor Gallery in New York on January 31, 1966, by Charles Hamilton, a reputable autograph dealer who vouched for their authenticity.

The purchaser of the letter that *Ramparts* eventually published was Penn Jones Jr., who paid $950 for the artifact. Ruby's younger brother, Sam, immediately contacted Jones, and confirmed that Ruby had previously admitted to writing the letter. With Jones' permission, *Ramparts* published most of the letter (33 pages in its original handwritten form) as Ruby wrote it, without correcting his errors in spelling, grammar or punctuation, without attempting to clarify its ambiguities, contradictions and evident factual errors. It should, Welch wrote, be remembered that Ruby never went beyond the eighth grade in school. In the letter, Ruby expressed sympathy for Oswald and also believed he was a patsy and placed the blame for Kennedy's murder on Johnson. The only one who gained anything at all from the murder of Kennedy was Johnson, Ruby wrote, and Johnson was "in a car in the rear and safe when the shooting took place. "What would the Russians, Castro, or anyone else have to gain by eliminating the President?" Ruby asked. "If Johnson was so heartbroken over Kennedy, why didn't he do something for Robert Kennedy? All he did was snub him."[206]

In April 1967, *Ramparts* published an opinion piece contributed by William Turner titled "The Plot Thickens." Turner wrote about New Orleans District Attorney, Jim Garrison (played by Kevin Costner in Stone's *JFK*), who

---

[206] Jack Ruby, "A Letter from Jail: The Letter," *Ramparts Magazine*, February 1967, p. 22.

had recently opened an investigation into Kennedy's murder. Garrison has complained that he had received absolutely no cooperation from the FBI; it refused, for example, to make available the results of its investigation of the enigmatic David Ferrie (played by Joe Pesci in *JFK*) immediately following the assassination. Ferrie and Clay Shaw (played by Tommy Lee Jones in *JFK*), whom Garrison believed figured prominently in the assassination scheme, were investigated and cleared by the FBI in 1963. Garrison's suspects also included Cubans. The possibility that agencies such as the FBI were not only snubbing Garrison, but trying to learn his moves in order to checkmate them had occurred to his investigators, who believed their phones had been tapped. Some skeptics, Turner noted, said that Garrison was trying to make political hay out of his investigation, and was aiming beyond it at the governorship of Louisiana. But by the same token, Turner explained, if his case were to fall flat, he would plunge into political oblivion. In truth, Turner wrote, Garrison seemed to possess "rare courage."[207] Garrison was obviously, Turned pointed out, "a tough, competent investigator," and it was the series of implausibilities in the Warren Report, such as the close spacing of the shots and the theory that one bullet penetrated both Kennedy and Connally, that first aroused his curiosity. Once into the twenty-six volumes of the report, Garrison had discovered the incredible number of loose ends to the investigation.

Garrison did not, however, Turner noted, believe there was an express conspiracy in government to suppress the truth. But he did believe there was a tacit understanding that to delve too deep might not be in the national interest. This was implicit in the premature conclusion made by J. Edgar Hoover, barely three weeks after Kennedy's murder, that Oswald and Ruby both acted independently and were not part of a larger conspiracy. *Ramparts* had furnished Garrison information suggesting

---

[207] William Turner, "The Plot Thickens," *Ramparts Magazine*, April 1967, p. 8.

that a Ruby employee was in New Orleans recruiting people to come to Dallas prior to the assassination. Garrison had thus not overlooked the possibility that Oswald was framed and that Oswald really was, as he declared the night he was arrested, a patsy.

In June 1967, *Ramparts* published an essay titled "The Inquest," written by Turner. "Grand conspiracies need not be grand," he declared. There need only be a few central figures in a position to manipulate, wheedle, dupe, blackmail, and buy the bit actors. This was, Turner wrote, the theory of New Orleans District Attorney Jim Garrison as applied to the assassination of President Kennedy. Garrison, the Louisiana populist, claimed to have discovered who killed Kennedy, who organized the plot, and what forces were involved in planning the various steps that led to the assassination. The government "establishment," Turner wrote, had given Garrison "the cold shoulder," and the FBI, which "cleared" two of his primary suspects, Ferrie and Shaw, immediately following the assassination, refused to release its information to him.[208]

Garrison was thus convinced that Oswald was not a triggerman, and that Ruby was the puppet of a more sophisticated master. Garrison was equally sure that the working level of the conspiracy was composed of rabid anti-Castro Cuban exiles in league with elements of the American paramilitary right. The concerted "establishment" effort to confine the events of the assassination to Oswald and Ruby, Turner wrote, suggested the Garrison thesis: a vertically integrated plot rising step by step into high echelons of government and the military-industrial complex.

On February 22, 1967, after preliminary, lengthy questioning by the New Orleans District Attorney's office and shortly before he was to be arrested by Garrison and charged with conspiracy to assassinate Kennedy, Ferrie was found dead in his apartment. The second major

---

[208] William Turner, "The Inquest," *Ramparts Magazine*, June 1967, p. 17.

figure in Garrison's probe was 54-year-old Clay Shaw, a retired executive director of the New Orleans International Trade Mart, which was alleged to be a CIA front. Garrison alleged that Shaw participated in a meeting with Oswald and Ferrie in which Kennedy's assassination was discussed. Charged with conspiracy by Garrison, Shaw was awaiting trial in June 1967. A third individual expected to figure prominently in the Garrison inquiry was Manuel Garcia Gonzales. The New Orleans D.A. office had come into possession of a photograph taken at Dealey Plaza just before the assassination that showed several Latin men behind the low picket fence at the top of the now famed grassy knoll. Many Warren Report critics believed one or more shots were fired from the grassy knoll area, and Garrison believed Gonzales was one of the men in the photograph. Gonzales had disappeared and had, Turner wrote, probably fled the country.

Garrison concluded that Oswald was, in fact, only a decoy – a patsy. Turner argued that the murder at Dealey Plaza had "all the earmarks of a paramilitary operation" and that the site was ideal: tall buildings at one end, at the other end was a grassy knoll projecting to within a stone's throw of the roadway and covered by foliage. It was the opinion of Garrison's investigators, and Turner, that the slowly-rolling Presidential limousine was trapped in a classic guerrilla ambush — with simultaneous fire converging from the knoll and from a multi-storied building. This was the "triangulation" that Ferrie had allegedly talked about during his meeting with Oswald and Shaw — a sniper in the rear position to divert the public's attention while the sniper in front "could fire the shot that would do the job."[209]

Garrison also asserted that Oswald was not a committed communist, but rather a CIA operative. "He was a revolutionary looking for a revolution," Turner wrote, "any revolution — and he found a cause with the CIA-sponsored paramilitary right wing planning the overthrow

---

[209] Ibid, p. 20.

of Castro."[210] The hand of the CIA had materialized repeatedly in Garrison's investigation, and he had implicated anti-Castro Cuban factions aligned with the American paramilitary right—both of which had been utilized by the CIA in its machinations to overthrow Castro. Since the assassination, Turner wrote, the thawing Cold War with the Soviet Union had been shoved into the background by the new "holy war" against communism in Southeast Asia. This little hot war had, he explained, enabled the military-industrial complex against which President Dwight Eisenhower warned Americans about during his farewell address to become the central institution in America's increasingly corporatist and militarized society. "The hawks in the Pentagon, whose wings barely fluttered during the Kennedy epoch," were, Turner wrote, "now in full flight, and the CIA, which Kennedy sought to cut down to size," had become an

---

[210] Ibid, p. 24.

indispensable instrument of U.S. foreign policy in Southeast Asia. The Texas oil and contracting industries had, he further elaborated, profited immensely from fueling the war machine and building its warehouses and docks. No wonder that Garrison, Turner concluded, who attributed the assassination to a "powerful domestic force," sat at the "vortex of that force."[211]

Ramparts published yet another essay written by Turner in September 1967 titled "The Press vs. Garrison." Turner noted that Walter Cronkite during a recently published four-night *CBS* special series on the Warren Report "expertly blended gimmickry, dubious experimentation and cherrypicked witnesses" to ultimately "rubber-stamp the Warren Report practically point by point without giving its critics a chance for specific rebuttal." A week before the premier of Cronkite's series, *NBC* had broadcast its own special, which Turner referred to as an "attack" on Garrison and his

---

[211] Ibid, p. 29.

assassination conspiracy probe. The charges and conclusions of both programs were widely echoed in the daily press. What Americans witnessed, Turner argued, "was a strange and dangerous new phenomenon in which the networks synthesized news — leaving it to the television/radio columnists to pass judgment on the accuracy of their exposition of evidence." Turner wrote that he could sense an urgency in both productions that betrayed "any pretense at objectivity." It was only when Garrison propounded a counter-theory to the Warren Commission Report, produced evidence to support it, and indicated that he would use the full powers of his office to prosecute the conspirators that "beads of sweat started rolling down Washington foreheads."[212]

Six months in the making, at a cost of a quarter million dollars, the *CBS* series hosted by Cronkite was, Turner argued, obviously designed to revitalize sagging public confidence

---

[212] William W. Turner, "The Press vs. Garrison," *Ramparts Magazine*, September 1967, p. 8.

in the Warren Report—polls showed that a meager thirty-five percent were true believers in the government's official accounting of the assassination of Kennedy. What Turner referred to as the "massive propaganda barrage" had been aided not only by *NBC* and *CBS*, but also by the press at large. Hugh Aynesworth of *Newsweek*, for example, wrote that Garrison was shamelessly preying on the vulnerability of homosexuals, and the *Associated Press* disseminated a tendentious series whitewashing the Report—the longest tome in *AP* history. As for *NBC's* "slanted coverage," Garrison offered the theory that *NBC* was owned by *RCA*, and *RCA* was one of the top ten government contractors. In a "grotesque twist," Turner concluded, the networks and press had not only convicted the prosecutor in a trial by media, they had also judged a court case before millions of viewers and thus possibly prejudiced the jurors who would hear the case. Such tactics, Turner lamented, smacked of desperation — and indicated that there was "much to hide."[213]

Turner contributed another essay titled "The Garrison Commission" in January 1968. Despite the mainstream American corporate media making Garrison out to be a publicity-seeking quack, Turner noted that his record as a New Orleans District Attorney was especially impressive. His office, Turner pointed out, had never lost a major case, and no convictions had been toppled on appeal because of improper methods. "It was not Cosa Nostra," Turner wrote, but "the majestic might of the United States government trying to keep him from his duty."[214]

Turner then went on to present Garrison's case in the pages of *Ramparts*, including tying Oswald to a meeting with Ferrie and Shaw at 544 Camp Street in New Orleans on September 16, 1963. The trio allegedly discussed the plot to kill

---

[213] Ibid, p. 12.

[214] William W. Turner, "The Garrison Commission," *Ramparts Magazine*, January 1968, p. 43.

Kennedy in intimate detail, including the importance of "triangulation." The closer Garrison seemed to get to fitting together all the pieces of the "assassination mosaic," Turner wrote, "the more desperate the attempt to squelch him became."[215] The behavior of U.S. Attorney General Ramsey Clark had, Turner suggested, been most conspicuous of all. On March 2, 1967, the day after Shaw was arrested, the attorney general announced that Shaw had already been thoroughly investigated by the FBI in 1963 and had been "cleared" of any complicity in the assassination. Three months later, after the world had been "noisily advised" that the prestigious FBI had found Shaw innocent, Clark sheepishly admitted that there had in fact been no investigation at all. The retraction, however, hardly caused a ripple in the press.

Then on October 14, 1967, *United Press International* quoted Clark as telling an audience of law students at the University of Virginia that

---

[215] Ibid, p. 66.

Garrison "took a perfectly fine man," Clay Shaw, "and ruined him just for personal aggrandizement," and that the Department would prosecute the New Orleans DA. Clark promptly issued a denial, and a Department spokesman lamely explained that Clark had "discussed this matter hypothetically in response to a question" asked by a student. But the most reasonable interpretation, Turner asserted, was that Clark let slip precisely what was on his mind. When news of the assassination probe first broke, Garrison declaimed in a burst of rhetoric, "Let justice be done though the heavens fall!" The heavens are still there, Turner concluded, but "Washington had come crashing down upon him."[216]

The murder of Robert Kennedy in the summer of 1968 fueled conspiracy-theory fires. In September 1968, *Ramparts* published an essay titled "Assassinations: Sirhan's Motives," contributed by Mahmoud Abdel-Hadi, who was

---

[216] Ibid, p. 68.

an Egyptian correspondent for *Akhbar Elyoum* in Cairo. "Unlike Lee Harvey Oswald," Abdel-Hadi wrote, "Sirhan Sirhan," a Palestinian, who had murdered Robert Kennedy a few months earlier, had lived to tell of his motivations — but he had vexingly chosen to remain silent. The only other potential source of information was his family, which had not spoken to the press. Abdel-Hadi was, however, granted access to the family.

His interview provided as many questions as answers, but suggested that Bobby Kennedy's unvarnished support for Israel was Sirhan's primary motive. Shortly after his arrest, he said he killed Kennedy on behalf of his country. Like the murder of his brother John five years earlier, controversy and conspiracy theories that suggested Sirhan did not act alone were widely circulated in the aftermath of his murder in Los Angeles as he closed in on the Democratic Party's nomination to be its candidate in the upcoming general election.

Abdel-Hadi's essay was followed in the September 1968 edition of *Ramparts* by another article written by Turner titled "Assassinations: Epstein's Garrison." Turner noted that Edward Jay Epstein's *Inquest* (1966) which exposed the rather shoddy inner workings of the Warren Commission and laid bare the tortured logic it finally employed to dispel notions of a conspiracy had become a bestseller. Yet Epstein had since emerged as one of Garrison's most fervid accusers. Epstein's "vehicle," as Turner put it, was *The New Yorker*. In the July 13, 1968 issue of that magazine, Epstein delivered what Turner referred to as a 25,000-word blast at Garrison, in which Epstein called the DA's investigation a "fraud."

However, to those familiar with the facts, *The New Yorker* article was, Turner asserted, "badly slanted."[217] Turner conversely quoted Philosophy Professor Richard Popkin of the University of California at San Diego, who had written the book *The Second Oswald* (1966) in

---

[217] William Turner, "Assassinations: Epstein's Garrison," *Ramparts Magazine*, September 1968, p. 8.

which he propounded the theory of an Oswald double. "I found it a queer mix of facts," Popkin wrote in reaction to Epstein's *New Yorker* piece, "half-facts, rumors and very dubious information from people hostile to Garrison."[218] Turner provided a convincing point-by-point rebuttal to Epstein's *The New Yorker* piece, which Turner argued was published at "an opportune time for Clay Shaw." Obtaining advance copies of Epstein's essay, his attorneys entered it as evidence before a three-judge federal panel that was hearing arguments that the DA was "conducting a reign of terror" and "persecuting" the defendant. The panel was, however, apparently unimpressed because it unanimously rejected the defense's argument and ordered the case to trial. "If Garrison does get his day in court," Turner concluded, a day Epstein had "struggled to deny him" — chances were his case would hold up better than "*The New Yorker's*

---

[218] Ibid, p. 8. See also Popkin's rebuttal to Epstein; "Garrison's Case" in *The New York Review of Books* (September 14, 1967).

brief for the defense."[219] Shaw was, to both Turner and Garrison's great dismay, found not guilty on all charges on March 1, 1969, after the jury had deliberated for less than one hour.

More than five years passed before *Ramparts* published another essay specifically pertaining to the murder of John Kennedy. The essay in question was published in November 1973, almost a decade after the assassination. It was titled "Dallas to Watergate: The Longest Cover-up," and was contributed by Peter Dale Scott, who was author of *The War Conspiracy* (1972). His essay on the Kennedy assassination and the subsequent Vietnam escalation was also included in volume five of the Gravel edition of the *Pentagon Papers* (1972).

The discovery of the Watergate break-in on June 17, 1972, had, Scott explained, led slowly but irreversibly to wider revelations about the government's use of crime. Most of the burglars arrested at the Democratic National Committee

---

[219] Ibid, p. 11.

offices in the Watergate complex had, he noted, been employed by the CIA in anti-Castro activities, and one of them — Eugenio Martinez — was still on a CIA retainer. Another, Frank Sturgis (alias Fiorini), had defied President Kennedy's ban on U.S.-based raids against Cuba, and continued them with the support of former Havana casino operators with strong links to organized crime. His activities immediately before and after the Kennedy assassination had made Sturgis suspicious in the eyes of some private assassination buffs, long before Watergate made him a public figure. E. Howard Hunt, the man chosen by Nixon's re-election team to mastermind the Watergate break-in, had served as political officer in the CIA's Bay of Pigs operation, which Richard Nixon had almost single-handedly pressed on the Eisenhower administration, and for which Nixon was the White House Action Officer. In connection with the Bay of Pigs, Hunt had proposed the assassination of Castro to his CIA superiors, and, according to some sources, continued to propose similar assassination projects, the latest of these against the President of Panama in 1971.

In Scott's opinion, it was no coincidence that the key figures in Watergate - Liddy, Hunt, Sturgis, Krogh, Caulfield — had been drawn from the conspiratorial world of government narcotics enforcement, a shady realm in which the operations of organized crime, counterrevolution, and government intelligence had traditionally overlapped. Nor was it a coincidence, Scott asserted, that one of these men — Watergate burglar Frank Sturgis — played a minor role in the cover-up of the Dallas assassination ten years earlier. Scott asserted that a full exposure of the Watergate conspiracy would help to understand what happened in Dallas, and also to understand the covert forces which later mired America in what he believed to be a "criminal war in Southeast Asia."[220]

---

[220] Peter Dale Scott, "Dallas to Watergate: The Longest Cover-up," *Ramparts Magazine*, November 1973, p. 12.

If Americans were to focus only on the ensuing Dallas cover-up, he argued, the evidence of conspiracy, and the identity of some of the principals, were unmistakable, as was the "central presence of criminal and intelligence networks also evident in the politics of Watergate and Vietnam."[221] Scott then cited an article published in a July 1973 edition of *The Atlantic* in which former President Lyndon Johnson likewise expressed doubts about the findings of the Warren Commission despite his public support of its "lone assassin" hypothesis. Interviewed not long before his death, Johnson expressed his belief that the assassination in Dallas had been part of a conspiracy. Johnson said that when he had taken office, he learned that the U.S. had been operating a "damned Murder Inc." in the Caribbean. A CIA-backed assassination team, Johnson recounted, had been picked up in Havana a year or so before Kennedy's death. Johnson speculated that Dallas

---

[221] Ibid, p. 13.

had been a retaliation for this thwarted attempt. Johnson's recollection was corroborated by E. Howard Hunt in his memoir on the Bay of Pigs. Hunt admitted to having personally proposed an attempt to assassinate Castro, and although he claimed that nothing came of his proposal, this was, Scott asserted, "not true." He noted that the CIA's assassins nearly succeeded, but were caught and executed in Havana on the day of the Bay of Pigs invasion.[222]

In December 1973, *Ramparts* editorial staff published an article titled "The Kennedy Assassination: A Decade of Unanswered Questions." Lee Harvey Oswald's first reactions upon capture, they reminded readers, did nothing to quench conspiracy theories that seemed to begin the moment Johnson was sworn in aboard Air Force One on November 22, 1963. Handcuffed and in tow, Oswald, the editors pointed out, had neither the "bravado of the fanatic nor the bewilderment of the innocent,"

---

[222] Ibid, p. 15.

but the "outrage" of someone who actually seemed to believe that he was being made a "patsy."

But by whom, the editors rhetorically asked readers, had Oswald been set up by? Oswald was, they wrote, condemned to be the "Sphinx" in whose stony face many sought answers and received only riddles in return. Oswald had no chance to elaborate before being shot by Jack Ruby. And Ruby, never brought to trial, was confined until his death, all the while pleading to be taken to a place of safety so that he could tell his full story. Whoever pulled the trigger that day at Dealey Plaza "set off a wildfire of doubts;" only later, as the questions multiplied along with the questioners, would this outbreak be controlled by insisting that such speculations were made of "wild paranoia."[223]

But just a few years earlier, the editors pointed out, such "paranoia" was considered anything but. Mark Lane's *Rush to Judgment: A*

---

[223] *Ramparts* editorial staff, "The Kennedy Assassination: A Decade of Unanswered Questions," *Ramparts Magazine*, December 1973, p. 42.

Critique of the Warren Commission's Inquiry into the Murder of President John F. Kennedy, which was first published in August 1966, was an immediate best-seller. Afterwards, more documentary evidence began to emerge, pointing toward Oswald's associations with U.S. intelligence organizations and right-wing Cuban exiles and anti-communists, and to Ruby's ties with the police, Teamsters, and organized crime. In September 1966, when Representative Theodore Kupferman of New York introduced a motion in Congress calling for a new inquiry into the assassination, his proposal won endorsement from Tom Wicker of *The Times,* the editors of *Life,* and other figures who could hardly be accused of wild paranoia. A Lou Harris poll in the fall of that year revealed that only thirty-three percent of the American people believed the cornerstone of the Warren Commission's Report—that Kennedy was killed by a lone assassin.

What might have been seen as paranoia a few years earlier, the editors wrote, turned out to be "the core of the Watergate affair." The

American people, the editors added, had learned (or should have) much about the nature of America's militarized society in the previous decade. "We slaughtered women and children in Vietnam and then covered it up," they wrote; "there was bombing in Cambodia and then a cover-up; there was massive espionage at Watergate and then a cover-up." Given the atmosphere in Dallas in 1963, the editors beseeched readers, and the admitted inadequacies of the Warren Commission Report, "was it not equally possible that the assassination of President Kennedy was followed by a cover-up?"

Watergate had proven, the editors asserted, that the way to the heart of a plot was through the efforts to conceal its existence. And in the cold light of what Americans had learned concerning its government in the preceding months during the Watergate investigation, it was clear to the editors of *Ramparts* that a reopening of the assassination investigation was in order, especially in view of the fact that more than one strand of evidence had led from the burglary in the Watergate to murder in Dallas. "The reason this must be done," the editors concluded, was not so much out of "loyalty to a fallen President who may not have deserved such devotion, but out of loyalty to the truth and concern for the uncovering of totalitarian tendencies existing beneath the surface of American government—before it was too late."[224]

Also in December 1973, *Ramparts* published an essay written by Maxwell Robach titled "Executive Action: Hollywood Rediscovers Politics." Robach began by elaborating all of the washed-up stars at John Ford's funeral. Ford's death appeared to be a watershed in terms of a changing of the Old Hollywood Studio System of which he was such a central figure since the 1920s. Jane Fonda, Robach noted, had been to North Vietnam; Marlon Brando had spurned the Academy Award in solidarity with the American Indian movement; the former wife of Donald Sutherland had been indicted for her

---

[224] Ibid, p. 44.

involvement with the Black Panthers; and the memories of Hollywood's dark days of blacklists, loyalty oaths and congressional snoopers had faded. In other words, the utopian fantasies commonly propagated by the Hollywood studio system were passé. Social realism was in vogue. Hollywood had, in short, begun to chart its own course back toward films of socially and politically relevant content that had all but vanished during the 1950s era a McCarthyism. One such film, Robach wrote, was *Executive Action* (1973), a conspiracy thriller about the assassination of John F. Kennedy, written by Dalton Trumbo, Mark Lane, and Donald Freed, and directed by David Miller, and starring Burt Lancaster and Robert Ryan, which was released during the Watergate Scandal.

On April 26, 2018, in compliance with the deadline set by President Donald Trump in October of 2017, the National Archives released 19,045 additional documents from the JFK assassination files. But instead of a full reveal some material was kept from the public due to "identifiable national security, law enforcement, and foreign affairs concerns, according to a White House memo. The full truth of John Kennedy's murder thus remains shrouded in mystery for the foreseeable future. And so long as there is mystery surrounding Kennedy's assassination as a result of the shrouding of evidence, questions and theories will continue to have a relevance and cultural force.

EPILOGUE

From 1962 - 1975 *Ramparts Magazine* was, as this book has elaborated, a relentless critic of American political and economic corruption, which the editors often depicted to be evidence of fascism deeply embedded in yet often overlooked in Cold War American society. Editors and contributors to the magazine consistently depicted the United States during the 1960s and early 1970s to be infected by crony capitalism, a dependence on oil, yet rife with poverty and scarcity, as well as corporate and political corruption, and corruption in the realm of education. America was also, many articles elaborated, fraught with a weaponized brand of law and order that served as context for the murder of John and Robert Kennedy. Together, these diabolical aspects of American life were, contributors to and editors of *Ramparts* often deduced, glaring evidence of fascism deeply embedded in but often overlooked by the mainstream American media.

Though the institutions that comprised mainstream society most often ignored the specter of fascism in Cold War America's corporatist, technocratic and militarist society, these entities unwittingly inspired a counterculture that championed the rights revolution of the 1960s and early 1970s.

www.ingramcontent.com/pod-product-compliance
Lightning Source LLC
Chambersburg PA
CBHW021132090426
42740CB00008B/755